Under Tw...

in

ANGOLA

ZIMBABWE
(Southern Rhodesia)

Shakawe

Tsodilo
Hills

Nokaneng

Tsau

Maun

Nata

NAMIBIA
(South West
Africa)

Rakops

Gweta

Francistown

Serowe

Pilikwe
Palapye

Mahalapye

Tshane

Molepolole

Mochudi

Grootkalk

Gaborone
Lobatse

Dar es
Salaam

Tshabong

Bok-
spits

REPUBLIC OF SOUTH AFRICA

Johannesburg

Cape Town

Sketch Map of Botswana

Under Two Flags in Africa

Recollections of a British Administrator
in the Bechuanaland Protectorate and
Botswana 1954 to 1972

by

George Winstanley

Blackwater Books
2000

Cover photograph: George Winstanley on a police camel at Lehututu in 1956. Photograph by MRB Williams.

ISBN: 0 953 9206 0 7

First published September 2000.

Published by Blackwater Books, 1 High Street, Kelvedon, Colchester, CO5 9AG.

Printed for Blackwater Books by Jenner (City Print) Limited of Tiptree, Essex.

FOREWORD

This book is not a history. It consists of personal recollections of my years in the Bechuanaland Protectorate and Botswana between 1954 and 1972 and for the most part it is light-hearted.

It is not meant to be a complete record. I never kept a diary and I have not consulted any archives so what is recorded is based on my memory which is fortunately very good when concerned with matters which have moved or amused me, as is the case with most of the material presented here. On two or three occasions I verified dates from *Seretse Khama 1921 – 1980* by Thomas Tlou, Neil Parsons and Willie Henderson (Macmillan, 1995). Some of the incidents that I write about were described to me and whilst I have accurately recorded these descriptions I cannot vouch for their veracity.

I am most grateful to Sandy Grant on behalf of the Phutadikobo Museum, Mike Williams, Lionel Palmer, John Wilson, and Noel Redman for generously allowing me the use of their photographs.

George Winstanley
August 2000

A NOTE ON PLACE NAMES

The spelling of place names such as Lobatse and Gaborone which were changed after independence from Lobatsi and Gaberones as well as of Mafikeng (formerly Mafeking) has been standardised to modern spelling. However the names of countries, including Bechuanaland (Botswana) are used in both forms according to the period which is being recalled.

CONTENTS

CHAPTER 1 Preparing for the Colonial Service *1*
    The Colonial Service interview *3*
    Pre-service training in London *6*
    By sea to Cape Town *8*
    Up country to Mafikeng *12*
    North by train *15*
CHAPTER 2 My first station *17*
    Learning the ropes in Francistown *19*
    Early experiences in court *22*
    On tour with the OC Police *26*
    Tales around the camp fire *30*
    District work *34*
    Searching for a lost aircraft *37*
    Continuing the search to Lake Dow and Rakops *39*
CHAPTER 3 South to Mahalapye *44*
    Coupon Lou *46*
    Introduction to Mahalapye *48*
    Seretse Khama and the chieftainship dispute *50*
    Meeting the Rutherfords *52*
    Tshekedi Khama *56*
    District work and pleasure *59*
    Around the bar at the Mahalapye Hotel *63*
    The Tuli Block *66*
    Preparing for Seretse's return *71*
    Seretse's return *75*
CHAPTER 4 The Kalahari *83*
    Station life *84*
    My friend Bok *90*
    On tour in the desert *92*
    Tshane *94*
    A visit to Mrs Bok *97*
    On tour in the Kalahari *99*
    School visits *102*
    In Court at Tshabong *105*

Kalahari ghosts *107*

A tale of a leopard *110*

CHAPTER 5 Posted to Ngamiland *116*

Ngamiland *121*

On tour in Ngamiland *126*

Ngamiland places and people *131*

Riley's Hotel *137*

The Kays family *141*

More Maun people *146*

Jock Allan and friends *151*

The old man and the cigarette *157*

Webby *162*

An outbreak of rabies *166*

CHAPTER 6 South to Lobatse *176*

The High Court *178*

Graveside tales *180*

A visit from Oliver Tambo *184*

Wedding bells *187*

CHAPTER 7 The Bakgatla *191*

A flogging *196*

Mochudi people *198*

Life at the Residency *200*

Dave Robinson *204*

CHAPTER 8 Transferred to Headquarters *211*

Headquarters work *213*

Executive Council *215*

Legislative Council *218*

CHAPTER 9 The first Elections and moving the Capital *223*

The new government *229*

Moving towards Independence *234*

Independence *238*

CHAPTER 10 The Ministry of Agriculture *242*

Another election *247*

A new Minister *249*

Moving on *252*

ILLUSTRATIONS

GW on board the 'City of Paris' 1954 *79*

A typical bush road in the Bechuanaland Protectorate *79*

The Residency at Molepolole in 1948 *80*

The police post at Rakops in 1947 *80*

Tshekedi Khama in London in 1930 *81*

A village school in the 1950s *81*

Chiefs Mokgosi and Bathoen, and Regent Tshekedi Khama in 1947 *82*

Bruce Rutherford and AO Wande in 1947 *82*

Aerial view of Tshabong in 1954 *112*

Tshane Pan *112*

The road from Tshabong to Tshane *113*

Headmen of the Kgalagadi District at Tshabong in 1955 *113*

GW on a police camel at Lehututu in 1956 *114*

The kgotla at Lehututu in 1956 *114*

A Bushman camp in the Kalahari *115*

On tour in the Kalahari *115*

Crossing the flooded Shashi river *170*

The causeway at Samadupi near Maun after floods *170*

Cattle crossing the Zambezi at Kazangula *171*

Ted Warren and Lionel Palmer in 1952 *171*

The Maun caboose team *172*

The caboose stuck in 'black turf' in Ngamiland in 1957 *172*

Regent of the Batawana, Mrs Moremi in 1958 *173*

Herero woman and baby *173*

Herero gathering in 1958 *174*

MRB Williams in Maun in 1958 *174*

Captain AC Webb (Webby) and Bushman women in the Kalahari *175*

Colonel Bob Langley with a mounted police escort *175*

The High Court building in Lobatse *190*

GW and Bridget in 1960 *190*

Mochudi in 1960 *208*

Chief Molefi of the Bakgatla in about 1937 *208*

Chief Molefi in 1945 *209*

Acting Chief Mmusi in about 1961 *209*
David Robinson in 1962 *210*
African Advisory Council in 1946 *221*
African Advisory Council in 1947 *221*
Tsheko Tsheko with GW in 1967 *222*
GW and Sir Hugh Norman Walker in 1966 *222*
Tsheko Tsheko talking to herdsmen *240*
Quett (later Sir Ketumile) Masire in 1966 *240*
Sir Seretse Khama, HRH the Princess Marina, Sir Hugh Norman
Walker and Lady Khama in 1966 *241*
HRH the Princess Marina and Sir Seretse Khama in 1966 *241*

CHAPTER 1

PREPARING FOR THE COLONIAL SERVICE

Soon after I began my last year at Cambridge in late 1952 I realised that I would have to give serious thought to life after graduation. A degree in geography did not automatically suggest a particular career but for some time I had been toying with the thought of working in Africa so I sent off to the Colonial Office for an application form. When I filled it in I thought I would increase my chances of being accepted if I widened my options so I put down the Administrative Service as my first choice and the Colonial Soil Survey as my second. I listed Uganda as the country of my preference and sent the form off.

About a month later I was summoned to the Colonial Office in London where I was interviewed by a man of about forty who was tweedy, moustached, pipe-smoking, and very tanned with piercingly blue eyes. He chatted on in a seemingly relaxed and casual manner but I knew I was being carefully appraised. After 15 minutes or so of courteous but penetrating probing he asked me why I had put down the Soil Survey as a choice and I said something innocuous in reply. He simply smiled and told me I wouldn't enjoy that life – "they live in tents" – and deleted my second choice from the form. He terminated the interview by telling me to let the Colonial Office know when I got my degree – "they like an upper second" – and I would then be called for interview by the Selection Board. I returned to Cambridge to coast along to the finals of tripos and an upper second.

Soon after this interview I was contacted by a wealthy American who was deeply interested in glaciers but was too old to study them in the field himself. He asked me to lead an expedition to the Monte Rosa glacier near Zermatt in Switzerland in the summer of 1953. He was interested in how ice moved and I had been on two expeditions to Norway in the Cambridge long vacations to study glacier movement and had corresponded with the American – hence the invitation. He asked me to recruit a team and I approached three friends who agreed to come.

Much to our surprise we discovered that we were to be paid – very generously – and given first class tickets to and from Zermatt. When we got there we were contacted by two young Swiss guides who eventually helped us to transport our kit up Monte Rosa because we planned to camp at about 15,000 feet whilst we spent our days digging a tunnel in the glacier until we reached the mountain wall. The guides visited us from time to time bringing supplies and we popped down to Zermatt about once a fortnight to wallow in hot baths and eat hugely. Our ablutions in camp were limited to washing hands and cleaning teeth and because we had to carry everything up the mountain on our backs food in camp was basic and sparse.

Before I left for Zermatt I had been instructed by the Colonial Office to present myself for interview on the 16th August. The days flashed by and the date of the interview drew near. Leaving myself a couple of days to spare I reluctantly left my friends still digging the tunnel in the ice and set off for England. During the weeks on Monte Rosa I had not kept up with any news. When I arrived at the Gare du Lyon in Paris I wondered why the station was so crowded so early in the morning. When I asked a gendarme in my appalling French why this was so he told me the country's railways were strikebound –"La grève monsieur."

Off I went to the British embassy to try and persuade someone to send a telegram to the Colonial Office but the embassy staff, who were besieged by stranded British tourists, had other things to attend to so I sent one myself. Some of the people besieging the embassy were quite desperate because they had very little money and they were literally marooned in Paris. I wasn't bothered about that because I was well supplied with money from the glacier and Paris had plenty of attractions for a 23-year-old. However, after three or four days the embassy arranged for motor coaches to take the stranded tourists to Calais and I was allocated a seat on one of them.

When I got to London I went straight to the Colonial Office and had some difficulty in convincing a porter there that I was a candidate for interview. Beards were not very common amongst young men in the early 1950s. He didn't think much of my rucksack and was very suspicious about my ice pick that he seemed to regard at worst as a lethal weapon or at best as a navvie's tool. However, he eventually accepted that I was not some eccentric tramp and arranged for me to see someone but he insisted on my leaving the offensive ice pick and rucksack with him – not that I wanted to hang on to them whilst wandering through the corridors of power in the Colonial Office.

A messenger conducted me to an office occupied by a rather forbidding looking woman who had what was obviously my file in front of her. She confirmed that my telegram had been received and gave me a date towards the end of August when the Selection Board would be sitting next. She put me down for 10.30 in the morning and, without actually saying so, gave me to understand that I had better not be late for this one.

The Colonial Service interview

I went up to London the day before the interview and, still flush with the glacier money, booked into a very good hotel. I thought this would put me in good spirits for the interview and it did. I was at the Colonial Office half an hour before the appointed time. The porter who regarded me with such suspicion on my visit earlier in the month was on duty but he didn't recognise me – or if he did he didn't let on. He even addressed me as "Sir" which I thought was rather encouraging.

When the time arrived I was taken to a room on an upper floor. The messenger opened the door and ushered me in but did not come in himself. The room was quite bare except for a curved table at the end about 30 feet away at which seven men were seated looking at me. There was an empty chair facing the curved row of interviewers. As I was advancing towards the Board I noticed that there was also an empty chair behind the curved table and I wondered why. The chairman rose as I neared the table and held out his hand. After I had shaken it he motioned to his right and left and said the others were his colleagues. I quickly decided against a general shaking of hands as none of them had moved and simply gave very slight right and left bows. With an almost imperceptible smile the chairman asked me to be seated.

He had just started the interview when I heard the door open and footsteps approaching. I immediately thought of the empty chair. When I glimpsed the newcomer out of the corner of my eye I deferentially stood until he had taken his seat. As he was doing so he smiled and courteously inclined his head. When I resumed my seat and caught the chairman's eye I knew that I had scored.

The first real question the chairman asked was why had I chosen Uganda as my preferred country and I replied that I had heard the climate was agreeable and the scenery wonderful. A gruff voice at the end of the table thought these were "damn poor reasons" and whilst I was groping for a polite but firm reply the chairman said he thought they were very good reasons indeed. I held my tongue.

The chairman then asked me what I had been doing in Switzerland. When I explained, the members of the Board seemed quite interested and I was asked two or three questions – didn't glaciers just slide downhill, wasn't it terribly cold camping at that altitude and how did we manage to wash ourselves. I replied without going into too much detail and tried not to appear boastful.

The chairman then said that he had once heard a tale about a very old woman who lived beside a glacier. She had chosen to live there because when she was in her late teens her lover, who was a guide, did not return from a climbing expedition to the upper reaches of the glacier and since then she had spent her life mourning her lost love. One morning when she was walking along the edge of the glacier she saw the perfectly preserved body of her handsome young man in the ice. I was asked whether I believed this.

I sat back in disbelief because when we were on the Monte Rosa glacier a young Zermatt guide came up the mountain one afternoon with an urgent message for Ernst – one of our guides. When they had finished talking Ernst immediately started packing his things. I asked the other guide what was going on and was told that Ernst's father, who had gone missing, had been found in the glacier. When I said that Ernst did not look very upset I was told that he could hardly remember his father because he had gone missing over twenty years previously. When Ernst returned to our camp about a week later he told us that his father was perfectly preserved and the spek in his haversack was still edible.

I hesitated briefly before telling this story to the Board because I thought the members might not believe me and think I was simply trying to cap someone else's story. However, they all listened with what seemed to be great interest. When I had finished the chairman thanked me and said that would be all – he didn't consult any of the other members – and I would hear from them in about a week's time.

I left feeling rather downcast because I thought I had failed the interview. Nobody had questioned me about my hobbies, what books I had read recently, who my favourite composer was or any of the usual stuff of interviews. I had arranged to meet a Cambridge friend for lunch. He was leaving for Nigeria the following week having been accepted into the Administrative Service there. When I told him about my interview and that I feared the worst he smiled and told me not to be a duffer.

He was right. A week later I received a telegram saying that subject to a satisfactory medical examination, I would be appointed to the Colonial Service, seconded to the Commonwealth Relations Office and posted to the Bechuanaland Protectorate to take up duties as an Administrative Officer (Cadet). Even though I had read geography at Cambridge I was uncertain where exactly Bechuanaland was and I had to consult an atlas. It looked a terribly empty place.

I had to have my medical examination at the School of Tropical Medicine in Liverpool and this, to me, seemed rather exotic – much more exciting that being examined by the local general practitioner. This was my first visit to Liverpool – the bomb damage was still very evident and it was pouring with rain. I was very pleased to be bound for Africa.

Pre-service training in London

Naturally, the medical posed no problem. I longed to get moving but I had to curb my impatience because, when I had been informed of my selection, I had also been told that I would be required to attend a course lasting one academic year at the London School of Economics. This course was known as the Devonshire Course because when it was first introduced a duke of that name was Colonial Secretary.

Devonshire courses were also held at Oxford and Cambridge and I was very disappointed that I had been allocated to the LSE which I regarded as a rather subversive institution. I had been allocated to London because I was required to learn the rudiments of Setswana, the main language of Bechuanaland, and a teacher was said to be available at the School of Oriental and African Studies but not at either of the other two universities. In fact this 'teacher's' knowledge of Setswana was rudimentary – he spoke a related language, Sesotho, very well. It was rather like being taught English by a Glaswegian. However, we managed, and the other course subjects – law, anthropology and economics – were very well taught by top-flight academics so my prejudice against the LSE was quite unjustified and I was ashamed of it.

I think the main purpose of the Devonshire course was to allow us to grow up before being let loose in Africa. Apart from the university lectures, we had talks by people home on leave from the various Colonies and Protectorates. One of the series of talks was by a man who must have been approaching seventy and who had been a District Officer in Tanganyika in the 1920s.

He used a blackboard when he wished to illustrate his lectures but he used it only as a support for his own illustrations which he had drawn in charcoal on the opened-out double sheets of old copies of The Times. He told us, amongst other things, how to draw maps, how to build roads and bridges with culverts, how to dig wells and latrines, how to make log paths when negotiating swampy ground by motor transport and how to make thorn enclosures to ward off wild animals. In the event, little of this information was of much use but we loved his 'Sanders of the river' approach and his charcoal drawings which were quite spectacular and obviously much used on many intakes of young cadets.

He also gave us useful tips on how to "look after ourselves". He had a phobia about dirty drinking water and what that could do to one's insides. He was particularly concerned to impress upon us the need to "keep up standards" especially on lonely one man stations, of the need to ration one's drinking to "never more than three a day", to have regular meals – breakfast, lunch and dinner – to shave every morning and, most particularly, to "always treat the local women with respect" and we understood his euphemistic way of saying what he meant.

We found all this rather amusing but we listened most respectfully to the old man because it would have been unthinkable to hurt his feelings. Later I came to appreciate that his advice was very sound and people who did not conform to his code of behaviour often ended up in a sorry mess.

The academic year in London was quite agreeable: I lived in a British Council residence near Harrods in Knightsbridge and so met young men from all parts of the world. I was rather well off because the Colonial Office put Devonshire Course students on three-quarters pay. However, I was so impatient to get out to Africa that the time seemed to pass awfully slowly. But at long last the course ended and I began to prepare for the ocean journey.

By sea to Cape Town

In those days – the early 1950s – the usual way of getting to Africa and all the other continents was by ocean liner. I was booked on an Ellerman & Bucknall ship called the City of Paris which, being an intermediate – that is to say it carried passengers and cargo – took three weeks to get to Cape Town from London instead of a mail ship's two. Packing for the voyage fuelled my growing excitement. The big trunk was labelled 'Not wanted on voyage' and the smaller cases with 'Cabin' stickers.

At long last in mid-August 1954 we set sail from London. It was heavenly. The cabin and catering staff were all Lascars and nothing was too much trouble for them. They went out of their way to be of service. When I was on deck waiting for the ship to cast off I took out a cigarette and put it in my mouth. Almost at once a brown hand holding a cigarette lighter flashed in front of me. When I went down to the cabin to unpack I couldn't find my suitcases at first. They were under the bunk and empty because someone had unpacked them. As I was sitting in the cabin marvelling at such pampering there was a gentle tapping on the door and the 'someone' appeared. He was a smiling teenager and was returning my newly pressed suits.

Life on board was leisurely and most pleasant. There were only about 40 passengers so nearly everybody was on speaking or nodding terms with everybody else. Two elderly spinster sisters took a great liking to me and seemed to lie in wait for me in their deck chairs to collar me for a chat. They were always knitting. They were on their way to join their missionary brother somewhere in Nyasaland. I got the impression that the older one had been engaged to someone who had not returned from the 1914-18 war and the younger one had sacrificed her life to be her companion.

The ship made only one landfall on the voyage to Cape Town. This was at Las Palmas and we had been told we would spend a full day there. In the event, because of some hold-up in the early part of the voyage, we didn't dock at Las Palmas until around midnight and we were told the ship would set sail at seven the next morning. This was disappointing because most of us were looking forward to going ashore.

I sounded out some friends, got together a party of six and we set off to explore the town. It was mainly in darkness – this was of course long before the days of package holidays. We managed to find a rather broken-down taxi and as the driver spoke no English apart from 'Hello' we had to convey to him by mime that we wanted to go to a place where we could get a drink and see some girls. We meant girls for dancing but I don't think we conveyed our meaning very accurately because the taxi driver immediately understood what we wanted and set off at a literally rattling speed.

We stopped in front of a large house that was in darkness. The driver got out and hammered on the door. A light came on, a window was flung open and a woman proceeded to have a shrill conversation with him. She withdrew and the lights came on downstairs and the front doors were thrown open. A plump, matronly Spanish woman welcomed us in with a smile to a sort of foyer. Her name was Madam Jesus. Quarter- and half-smoked cigarettes were in most of the ashtrays and some had been ground out on the floor.

I was beginning to worry about the nature of the establishment because our party included a newly married couple and the wife was strictly Welsh chapel. However it was too late to retreat because there was a rustling and half a dozen women swirled into the room. They were young and very pretty and wearing revealing clothes. They didn't seem to mind being roused out of their sleep. Madam Jesus spoke some English and the girls weren't put out when it was conveyed to them that all we wanted was to have a few drinks with a bit of dancing thrown in. Wine was produced and a wind-up gramophone brought into service. Mrs Welsh chapel was sitting petrified and very upright but seemed to cheer up when I told her she was one of the very few virtuous women who had seen the inside of a bordello. Her husband seemed to be enjoying himself.

After a very pleasant hour or so we paid Madam Jesus for the hospitality we had enjoyed and were given a cheerful send off by her vivacious girls. On the way to the docks we stopped at a café which was just opening and had some coffee. There were postcards on sale so I sent one home telling my parents that it was dawn in Las Palmas and I was enjoying coffee having just come out of a brothel. I was later to get a stern, lecturing letter from my father.

We got back on board safely and I went to bed. I woke at noon and was making my way to the bar when I spotted the spinster sisters in their deck chairs and, as always, knitting. Before I could dodge out of sight one of them saw me and waved me over. I was asked whether I had been ashore and I made some uneasy reply. The probing continued until one of them unable to contain herself said she had heard I had visited a "house of ill repute". The click of the knitting needles stopped as I began to reply and I realised they were both deeply interested. So I gave them a full account – stamped out cigarettes, Madam Jesus, scantily clad girls, dancing, castanets and wine. They listened intently with their heads bowed over their furiously clicking needles. When I left them for my drink in the bar I was still their favourite son.

On the journey out I had been told frequently that the Cape was delightful and that I had better make the most of my brief stay there because after the peninsular and its immediate hinterland all was desolation. Several people told me Bechuanaland was flat, empty, desolate and dull and they obviously pitied me so much that my natural optimism began to falter and I began to wonder what I had let myself in for.

Nevertheless, as we approached the Cape my excitement mounted and on the day we were due to make our landfall I was up before dawn to make sure I got an early glimpse of the magical Cape Peninsular. It was pouring with rain and everything was shrouded in mist. We docked at about nine in the morning and it was so cold and wet that I was very glad the train for the north left at two that afternoon.

On my first visit to Cape Town I didn't even see Table Mountain. I didn't see any black people either – I saw whites and 'Cape Coloureds'. There was plenty of evidence of discrimination against the latter. It was puzzling to my fresh mind why they were treated as inferior citizens because in appearance they looked to me like the inhabitants of Las Palmas and the ones I spoke to were cheerful and friendly.

Up country to Mafikeng

The train pulled out on time and I couldn't tear myself away from the window. The scenery was spectacular and as we drew away from Cape Town the rain eased off. The little huts that frequently occurred in clusters by the side of the railway line fascinated me. I saw little activity around them and thought they must be chicken houses although I saw no evidence of any chickens. When the conductor came round I asked him what they were. By the way he looked at me I am sure he thought I was bent on mischief but he must have decided I was genuinely puzzled and he told me they were huts for the labourers.

We were still going through marvellous country when night fell and after my first dinner in Africa I turned in because it had been a very long day. When I woke next morning it was just getting light. I tumbled out of bed and put up the blind. I half expected to see the mountains and the greenery of the night before but I was totally surprised by the landscape. It was flat, golden brown and barren with isolated flat-topped hills that broke the monotony from time to time. It was mainly empty but occasionally there was a homestead that seemed to be miles from anywhere and served to emphasise the utter loneliness of the landscape. I was profoundly moved by it. It was stark, positively beautiful and awe-inspiring. I thought of Keats and stout Cortes and his wild surmise. It was what the people on the ship had warned me against!

I spent the whole day watching the flat landscape roll by. The coal-powered engine chugged northwards on the narrow gauge track at no great speed making frequent stops so there was plenty of time to absorb every detail of the unfolding country-side. When we were well into the Northern Cape there was more evidence of cattle farming and homesteads. The humped and large-horned deep red cattle were new to me but then so was almost everything else that was passing before my fascinated gaze.

The train arrived in Mafikeng late that evening. This was my destination because, although it was in the Union of South Africa, it was by an historical accident, coupled with bureau-cratic inertia, the capital of the Bechuanaland Protectorate – or rather the splendidly named 'Imperial Reserve' was and this was on the rim of the town. This was where the Secretariat was situated – where the Resident Commissioner and the heads of the various government departments – Education, Veterinary Ser-vices, Police etc – and their staffs had their offices.

A jovial administrative officer, Dennis Atkins, who was meeting his wife off the train met me. She had been on a visit to Cape Town and although I had not bumped into her on the train, she knew all about me because she had shared a table in the dining car with the two old ladies who were bound for Nyasaland and they had apparently been complimentary about me.

Her husband soon spotted me and took me to the house of the Lawrensons. He was a senior Secretariat officer whose guest I was to be for a couple of days. My hosts seemed rather amused at my excitement over everything I had seen but they were very kind. They were obviously very fond of 'the BP' as they called the Protectorate and I was encouraged by the fact that after nearly 30 years in the Government service they were still enthusiastic and had a great affection for the country and its people.

I spent the next two days being shown around the various offices. Everyone was friendly and welcoming. The Resident Commissioner – Forbes Mackenzie – was a very tall and rather forbidding-looking man but he too was most kind and took me off to Protectorate House, which was his official residence, for lunch. On the way he stopped the car outside a vegetable shop to buy some avocado pears and to my confusion and embarrassment I didn't know what they were. He laughed hugely but not unkindly at my ignorance. At some stage during lunch he said that he had heard that I had been very popular on the ship coming out and I realised that news travelled fast in these small communities.

That evening before being put on the train to go north into the Protectorate I was handed over to Peter Fawcus, the Resident Commissioner's deputy, known as the Government Secretary, who gave me dinner and later took me to the station. He and his wife were most kind, welcoming and informal and so interested in me that I knew I was going to enjoy life in the Government service.

North by train

The train left Mafikeng around ten o'clock and I was asleep when we crossed the border. When I was wakened by the bedding boy bearing a cup of coffee we were well into Bechuanaland. This 'boy' was in fact a man old enough to be my father and we had a pleasant chat. He told me he lived in Cape Town and I deduced he was a Cape Coloured which is why he was referred to as a 'boy'.

The train was trundling north through country that was flat, brittle, dry, tawny coloured, dusty and studded with acacia bush. It seemed to stretch away to endless and empty horizons. I could understand why some people found it unattractive and hostile but to me it conveyed an expansive sense of peacefulness. Here and there were herds of well-scattered cattle and tighter flocks of small stock – mainly goats. Now and again smiling boys and girls waved at the passing train. The train stopped quite frequently at what were known as halts and black people got on whilst others got off but this activity took place far away in another part of the train. Racial segregation was total. The only non-white people in my part of the train were servants.

We passed alongside several quite large villages that consisted of thatched mud huts surrounded by mud walls enclosing small courtyards that were areas of domestic activity. There were usually a few larger buildings painted white with corrugated iron roofs. I was told these were trading stores. In these villages and around them there was not a blade of grass and as there was a stiff breeze blowing, everything was very dusty. The 'roads' were simply unsurfaced tracks. They were totally unlike English villages. They were yellow, dusty and harsh. I was spellbound.

The train stopped at each of these villages and at one of the larger ones it took on coal and water so I was able to get off and walk around. The village was called Mahalapye. I thought this was a very exotic name. There was a small hotel adjacent to the station platform with the bar opening on to it. Alongside the bar and behind it was a rather dusty but nevertheless attractive garden and behind that were bedrooms for hotel guests. In the garden there was a circular cemented area about 30 feet across. I was told by someone sweeping up that in the evenings when the mail trains stopped to take on water and coal, dances were held to a gramophone and the circular area served as the dance floor. I went into the bar and had a beer. The barman was very friendly. There was a stuffed head of a young lioness on the wall. The barman told me that he had shot it. I thought this was a pity but I didn't say so.

As we steamed north the vegetation changed. The thorn bush gave way to mophane veldt which was rather monotonous but which, so the bedding 'boy' informed me, was good cattle country. Although the mophane bush was ragged looking, tall umbrella-shaped thorn trees added variety and beauty to the landscape. Now and again the flatness was relieved by low-lying hills. It was all very dry and from time to time we crossed over rivers of sand. One of the stewards told me that in the wet season these became raging torrents of yellow water. I tried to imagine what the country would look like when it rained and all the yellows and browns changed to green.

CHAPTER 2

MY FIRST STATION

Early on a Saturday afternoon I arrived at my destination. It was a dusty little settlement called Francistown. All the roads were unmetalled. Parallel to the railway track was a line of trading stores and two hotels – one called the Grand and the other the Tati. Outside the Tati Hotel was a hitching rail. I could see all this from the train. The town looked exactly like something out of the Wild West.

A short, rather plump man wearing tinted spectacles met me at the station. He was dressed in khaki shorts and bush jacket and was wearing a topee. He was the District Commissioner, George Atkinson, and was to be my superior officer. He took me off to his bungalow because I was to spend the first few days with him and his wife until I got my luggage sorted out.

After we arrived at the house and I had been shown my bedroom, my host said he was going to take his afternoon nap. His wife was nowhere to be seen so I assumed that was what she was doing. I was too green to be 'afternoon napping' so I slipped out of the house and walked around the bungalows that made up the 'Government camp.'

It was ferociously hot but the houses, with their large wrap-round verandahs – locally called 'stoeps' – promised coolness and comfort. I heard a bird calling from a thorn tree. It had a long, drawn-out call that sounded like "go-away." It was a grey loerie and its harsh, creaking call seemed to reflect the crackling mid-afternoon heat.

However, the gardens were very 'English' apart from the

exotic flowers growing in them and in most a youngish black male was moving slowly about tending the garden. At the side and to the rear of the houses I could see little groups of black women in uniforms – usually blue – sitting chatting and often knitting – some were casually but carefully tending white babies. Others were folding clothes from what I presumed was the just-finished ironing. They all seemed to be cheerful and were chatting happily but quietly so as not to disturb the peace of the afternoon.

The government camp skirted a kopje (a lowish flat topped hill) consisting mainly of boulders piled on top of each other. I thought I would climb this to get a better view of the surrounding countryside. The view from the top fascinated me. The sky was cloudless and the flat plains of northern Bechuanaland stretched out into the distance. Everything shimmered in the afternoon heat but there was a slight breeze blowing that, although warmish, was refreshing. There were numerous dassies – rock hyrax – scurrying about on the rocks and disappearing in the crevices at the first hint of danger. When I was clambering back down I was alarmed by a crashing noise in the bushes and to my astonishment a kudu bull leapt across my path and bounded away.

When I got back to my host's bungalow it was time for tea and I was introduced to his wife who was obviously finding the heat very trying but she was gracious and welcoming. My host was amazed when I told him I had climbed the kopje and was not even wearing a hat! He was interested in the kudu bull. A small three-year-old girl wearing an old fashioned bonnet – the daughter of the house – was playing in a little canvas swimming pool on the lawn. We sat in the shade of a large tree and had tea and scones.

As the evening drew on it became cooler and after showering

and changing, we had sundowners on the lawn then dinner. After that my host said he would take me down to see the town at night. There was in fact very little to see apart from the two hotels and the closed trading stores in a line between them. We first passed the Grand Hotel and my host had to drive very slowly because outside a hall that was attached to the main hotel building there was a large crowd of black people. Many were standing on tiptoe. I asked what was happening and was told they were trying to watch the Saturday evening film show which was being screened in the hall – the doors were wide open because it was hot. I asked why they didn't go inside to watch because they could not have heard any sound outside. My host said the film show was for whites only.

We stopped at the Tati Hotel and went in for a drink. There were quite a few people in the bar – all men, all white, all very tanned and most dressed in khaki clothes. My host was greeted with great respect and when I was introduced to one man after another, my hand was repeatedly crushed with hearty friendliness. We were offered many drinks but we slipped away as soon as we could without appearing rude. I could see that my host was not at ease with the hearty, heavy drinking types in the bar and that he had screwed up his courage to take me there.

Learning the ropes in Francistown

I soon settled in and the District Commissioner kept a strict eye on me. I shared an office with him and used to surreptitiously watch him closely because he fascinated me. Referred to as Atters by most people but not by me or any of his subordinates, he was very shy and self-effacing and I frequently puzzled over why he had chosen the Colonial Service as a career. He arrived at and left the office exactly on time carefully changing his spectacles each time so the tinted ones were worn outside and the clear ones inside. He didn't like the heat and the dust and he hated flies. He had a fly whisk made out of the tail of a wildebeest and he wielded it viciously and accurately. I would watch fascinated whilst he froze, often in mid-conversation, and stealthily raise his whisk into a fly-killing position before delivering the *coup de grace* to some insect.

One morning I was a bit late getting to the office because I had celebrated well but not wisely the night before – I had certainly ignored the three drinks advice. I crept in and was greeted rather icily. I pulled out the tax register that I was revising – a deadly boring task – and pretended to be hard at work but in fact I was half asleep. I was startled into wakefulness by a stinging switch to the side of my head. I thought I was being punished but it was only the fly-hunter claiming another victim.

One Sunday afternoon soon after I arrived in Francistown, I decided to go for a drive in my new Chevrolet pick-up truck which was standard issue to young cadets like me so we could get out 'on tour'. I was still learning to handle it on the bush tracks that were sinuous and very sandy in places. Around Francistown there was a farming block consisting of small farms owned by what were called 'Europeans' despite the fact that all of them were either Rhodesians or South Africans.

I was about to pass one homestead that was just off the road when I thought I would be sociable and call in. I pulled up and the farmer – a burly South African called Blackie Mynhardt – was sitting on the stoep. He beckoned me to join him and when I did I noticed there was a whisky bottle on the table in front of him with what looked like a very stiff one in his glass. Blackie told me he didn't usually drink at five o'clock in the afternoon but he had just been bitten in the head by a big snake and because he judged he would never make it to the hospital 20 miles away he thought he might as well have a last drink before he met his Maker.

He said he was surprised he was still alive because he had been bitten 20 minutes earlier. He had been working in one of the farm sheds and when he pulled a plank from the rafters he saw the snake strike and ducked but it clipped the top of his head. One of the labourers had killed it with a knobkerrie and it was laid out in the yard next to the verandah. It was about six feet long and Blackie told me it was a black mamba. This snake has a deadly poisonous bite, its victims usually dying soon after being bitten.

We sat there and nothing happened so after a while I joined him in a sundowner. He was very puzzled. He certainly had been bitten and invited me to feel his bite which I did rather gingerly. After a few drinks he concluded that the snake must have killed just before it bit him and so had emptied its poison sacs. We drank to his deliverance. He became a very good friend of mine and bore the scar from the bite on the crown of his head – two slight bumps – forever after. When I met up with him from time to time after absences, feeling his bumps became a ritual.

In addition to getting to know the people and making friends I had to learn the ropes as a Cadet District Officer. I dealt with most of the petty business. Once a young African woman complained that she had been dismissed without pay from her job as a 'wash-girl'. After I had listened to her story I sent a note to her previous employer asking her to come to my office to settle the complaint against her. She did so with ill grace. She was youngish, pinch-faced, cigarette-smoking and rather slovenly. She said she had dismissed the 'native' because she was a thief. I asked what she had stolen and was told "a bucket of hot water." The dismissed servant was paid not only for the days she had worked but for the remainder of the month as well. Her previous employer left the office in a bit of a huff and when I looked across to the District Commissioner he had a slight smile – I think of approval – on his face.

Early experiences in court

An important part of my duties consisted of court work and to start me off the District Commissioner required me to sit in on cases when he was presiding. He was very good in court. He knew his law well and, because he was a humane person, he administered justice fairly.

On one occasion he was dealing with a very unpleasant individual. He had an Irish name but I think several other nationalities had co-operated in his make up. He was charged with wife-beating and I gathered this was his favourite sport when drunk which was frequently. The evidence in the form of a youngish woman of mixed race was in court and she had been badly beaten about the face by her drunken husband. The District Commissioner found the accused guilty and told him what he thought of him. He then gave him a prison sentence because he had previous convictions for the same offence. The prisoner started hurling foul abuse from the dock threatening all sorts of bodily harm against the District Commissioner who, being alarmed, hurriedly adjourned the court and made a swift exit through the door behind his chair before anyone else in the court could move.

However, the policeman who was prosecuting, Sub-inspector Norman Towell, had other cases to bring before the court. He darted after the departing District Commissioner who, on hearing footsteps pounding across the wooden courtroom floor and thinking it was the person he had just sentenced, grabbed hold of the door handle and hung on for dear life while urging who he thought was his potential assailant to calm down and think of the consequences of his actions. After a bit of shouting and tugging on either side of the door, the Sub-inspector established his presence, order was restored and the rather flustered District Commissioner returned to the bench to attend to the remaining cases.

One morning shortly after this incident I was alone in the office when the police prosecutor, Sub-inspector Alan Tilbury, appeared at the door and asked where the District Commissioner was. I told him he had gone to Bulawayo for the long weekend that was coming up. The Sub-inspector then told me that there was a case to be tried and I would have to do it. I protested in great alarm because although I had sat in on several trials, actually conducting one was rather different. He told me not to worry, the case was one of petty theft but it had to be dealt with because the only witness had to leave for the south that afternoon and I would be guided through the proceedings.

So I nervously slid through the door and climbed into the presiding officer's chair. The people below me seemed a long way off but we got going. The Sub-inspector presented an immaculate case and when he had finished I told the accused I found him guilty as charged. The prosecutor hastily scrambled to his feet and with great deference – actually addressing me as "Your worship" – asked me whether I would care to hear if the accused had anything to say in his defence.

But I soon gained experience and took on the main burden of the court work. The District Commissioner didn't like presiding in court so he appeared on the bench to hear serious cases only. My judicial powers were limited because I was a Cadet.

Some of the cases were very tedious especially those involving the theft of small stock – usually goats. Witness after witness would testify about the colour and parentage of the stolen goat or goats so as to prove ownership and there would be long wrangles between the accused and the witnesses. The courtroom was usually very hot and stuffy. The witnesses who had often come in from outlying villages had invariably brought many flies with them and pungent aromas. I would sit there suffering in coat and tie – essential elements of British dignity – brushing the flies away and patiently trying to unravel the squabble before me.

Even though my judicial powers were limited I was allowed to preside over preparatory examinations which sought to establish whether a crime had been committed – the crimes involved were usually cases of alleged murder. The decision whether to prosecute or not was taken by the Attorney General in headquarters after he had studied the papers sent to him. If a prosecution was proceeded with a court of appropriate jurisdiction handled it.

One of the preparatory examinations I presided over involved a case of ritual murder. The headman of a remote village in the interior, in league with a witch doctor, had allegedly murdered a Bushman and used various parts of his body – mostly the fat – for medicine to make the village cattle fertile. An important part of the evidence involved the identification by a Bushman witness of the footprints – the spoor – of the headman at the place of the alleged murder. He – the headman – denied ever being near the place. It wasn't crucial evidence but, at the prosecutor's suggestion, we decided to test the witness.

We lined up about 20 prisoners down one side of the prison compound. The ground was baked hard but had a light dusting of blown sand over it. We then got the prisoners who were spaced about two feet apart in line to walk across the compound. The headman was in the line. They were then marched away and the witness produced from around the corner. He walked down the starting line and without any hesitation whatsoever picked out the headman's spoor and followed it across the compound. We repeated this experiment twice more and the witness scored each time. I could see nothing on the ground except very faint and intermittent scuffs.

The headman and the witch doctor were later convicted in the High Court – on evidence in addition to the spoor recognition – and in due course were hanged. I was told that on the very day that the witch doctor was hanged, his hut which was about 600 miles away from the central gaol, was struck by lightning. The hut might well have been destroyed in this way but I suspect that the timing of the two events – the lightning strike and the hanging – became shorter in the telling to bolster local superstition.

On another occasion I thought I was about to witness an assault on a witness by a police inspector who was conducting the case for the prosecution. It was a preparatory examination into an alleged murder. The witness had given his evidence. I had recorded it in writing and then read it back to him to satisfy him that I had accurately recorded what he had said. He was required to certify the statement he had made and, as he was illiterate, his thumbprint had to be affixed to it and witnessed. He was a simple old man and I could see that he found the proceedings very strange and confusing.

The police inspector, who was a bit of a martinet, was dressed in his number one uniform complete with gleaming Sam Browne belt. I suppose he thought the case was serious – which it was – and he was dressed for the solemnity of the occasion. I privately thought he was a rather tiresome man.

He produced an inkpad and speaking Setswana (he was an excellent linguist) asked the old man for his right hand. The bewildered witness held out his hand and the inspector grabbed hold of the thumb by the base and pressed it on the pad. He then lifted it up, looked at it, and being a perfectionist, must have decided it would not produce a good impression – possibly because it was over-inked or a piece of lint was adhering to it. Whatever the reason he told the old man to wipe his thumb.

The witness was by now completely bewildered and stood with his thumb in the air as though hitching a lift. The inspector repeated his instruction and for the sake of clarity accompanied his order by wiping his own thumb down the front of his uniform. From the bench I could see exactly what was going to happen and it was then that the assault almost occurred because the poor old man wiped his thumb with a downwards sweep on the inspector's tunic leaving a long black streak.

On tour with the OC Police

One day the Officer Commanding the police in the Francistown district came into the office and told the District Commissioner that he was going on tour the following week to inspect a police sub-station about 100 miles west of Francistown. He said he would like to take me along to give me my first taste of the bush and permission was granted. The OC, Geoff Taylor, was an old-timer and had joined the police the year before I was born. He said he would pick me up at around six on the morning of the appointed day. I was up and waiting at five in case I missed him.

Off we set with a smart policeman driving, me in the middle and the OC on the window side of the front seat. The OC's orderly – another smart young black policeman – was in the back of the truck which had a canopy. We soon cleared Francistown and were travelling through the mophane woodland of northern Bechuanaland. It was cool and fresh but one could sense it was going to be a hot day.

After about an hour we saw a darkish patch on the road about a hundred yards ahead. It was a flock of guinea fowl – the first I had seen. The OC told the driver to slow down and coast along gently. Meanwhile he had wrestled a shotgun from behind the seat. When the truck stopped he sprang out and without further ado fired into the flock whilst it was still grounded and bagged two birds. He seemed quite pleased with himself and when I asked him whether that was a sporting thing to do he said he was more interested in dinner than in being voted gun of the year and that once the birds got into the bush they were impossible to bring down. I was learning fast.

We trundled on at no great speed because although we were on what passed as the main road it was little more than a wide track with frequent potholes. From time to time there were stretches of corrugations over which the truck shuddered and slewed. After a couple of hours we made a small detour to a village where there was a trading store. A kind-looking, avuncular man with snowy white hair greeted us warmly and insisted on giving us a cup of tea.

We took this at the counter because he was sitting on a chair behind it watching over the till and supervising the activities of his shop assistants. It was a general dealer's store in the exact sense of the words. An amazing variety of goods – foodstuffs, cooking utensils, plough chains and clothing – were being offered for sale. On the wall behind the till was a huge poster with a diagram of a naked man in black and red outline displaying all his various organs in lurid detail. A little box inset near the lower regions gave the equivalent female organs. Arrowed lines leading from the various organs gave the name of the patent medicine guaranteed to cure any defect in the organ in question. I thought someone was making much money out of ignorance as most of the quack medicines on sale were probably useless. We finished our tea and left the hospitable storekeeper to his general dealing.

Just after noon the OC said it was lunch time. We drew off the road when we spotted a large tree with deep shade. The orderly produced a canvas water basin, soap and towel. We washed our hands and faces and then retired to the camp chairs that had been set up alongside a table. The police captain produced a bottle of gin, a bottle of bitters and collected the canvas water bag which had been hanging on the side mirror of the truck since we left Francistown, gently oozing water and cooling the contents. He poured two enormous pink gins – one for each of us – and sat down with a sigh of profound contentment.

After a few big sips he told the orderly to bring out the lunch. This consisted of corned beef thickly sliced and two large raw onions, peeled and halved. He told me that this was his favourite lunch but he could never get it at home. This didn't surprise me but it was amazingly good!

We carried on through the hot afternoon. I was feeling well-fed and rather drowsy because of the unaccustomed gin in the middle of the day. At about four o'clock we came to the Nata river which in fact was a river of sand. The police post was about two miles 'upstream' of the drift. We saw the Union Jack flying proudly in the hot, stiff breeze from about half-a-mile distance and the driver was told to stop. The orderly appeared from the back of the truck and helped the police captain to change into his No.1 uniform complete with Sam Browne and shoes gleaming with ox-blood polish. We then drove on.

The police post consisted of two mud huts each roughly 20 feet square with corrugated iron roofs. These were the offices. Behind them were two rows of round mud huts with thatched roofs – these rondavels were the staff houses. The entire area was surrounded by a stockade of cut thorn bushes to keep out the goats. There were plenty of whitewashed stones and although everything was sandy and dusty the general effect was of efficiency and authority.

The little contingent was waiting to receive their OC who, on alighting from the truck, first saluted the flag then walked smartly across to where the policemen were lined up. There were five black troopers under the command of a tall, fine-looking black corporal. They were brought up to attention and the OC was received with a crisp salute from the corporal. Their faces were shining, their teeth gleaming, their brass buttons flashing in the sun and their uniforms were starched to immaculate perfection. I realised why the OC had done his men the courtesy of himself appearing on parade immaculately dressed.

After the inspection was over we carried on upstream for a mile or so until we came to a large wild fig tree. This was the camping site that was always used on inspections of the police post. We didn't bother with tents because it was the dry season: the orderly and the driver spread a large tarpaulin on the ground and set up the tables and chairs, the camp beds and the canvas wash basin. They then lit a huge fire – there was dead wood all around – hung the canvas water bag on a low branch and camp was established. All this had taken no time at all.

The OC fished a bottle of Cape brandy – "dop" he called it – from his trunk and we sat down to enjoy the sunset. The orderly had already plucked the guinea fowl – he must have done this on the journey – and he jointed them and popped them into a big three-legged, black, iron pot that he put on the fire. I noticed that it had "Made in Falkirk" embossed on the lid. He added water and, after the guinea fowl had been cooking for a little while he added onions, carrots and potatoes and the stew was under way. He then produced another pot and proceeded to make a stiff porridge out of maize meal. He had kept some of the guinea fowl to one side for himself and the driver and he cooked these pieces in a separate pot. All of this was done without any instructions being issued.

Darkness crept over the camp as we sat waiting for the stew to cook and drinking our dop with the water out of the bag that tasted slightly of canvas. There was a village a mile or so away and sounds from it drifted through the bush. Snatches of song and shouted conversation reached us. We could hear the village dogs yelping with pain after being hit with some missile for getting too close to the cooking pots. We could hear the velvety sound of the odd cowbell and now and again the high pitched, mocking, yelping of jackals as they scavenged round the village.

Tales around the camp fire

The stew was delicious and after we had eaten, the orderly made up the fire and we sat round it. The OC started telling me stories about Bechuanaland and I was enthralled. He told me the avuncular storekeeper we had met that morning was quite a lad with a great liking for the local girls and the bottle. His nephew, who owned a chain of trading stores and one of the hotels in Francistown was a member of the embryonic parliament and found the old man's antics very embarrassing.

The old man was once hospitalised for some complaint or other – probably drink-related – and during his convalescence decided he had had enough of sobriety and chastity so he decided to discharge himself. Very early one morning he set off for the town with its hotels which was about half a mile away. A nun who was also a nursing sister in the hospital spotted him scuttling through the hotel grounds clad only in his pyjama trousers. She shouted to him to come back but he ignored her and was soon over the fence, across the railway line and on the road to freedom. Grabbing her bicycle she set off in pursuit and caught up with him outside the Grand Hotel. There were very few people about because it was so early but one witness to the struggling nun and the half-naked patient heard him tell her to "leave me alone woman, you're making an exhibition of yourself".

He lived in a rondavel in the hotel grounds and just after sunrise one morning he caused consternation amongst the cleaners who were going about their duties, by standing in the doorway exposing himself and bawling out lewd invitations – he was of course well in his cups at the time.

The nephew decided enough was enough and that Francistown with its attractions was not the place for the old man so he banished him to a distant trading store and gave the staff strict instructions that he must not be supplied with liquor. I don't suppose he could do much about the local girls.

Once when the nephew went to inspect the store he noticed his uncle was rather merry and questioned the staff who swore they had obeyed his instructions. After a while he noticed the old man was paying frequent visits to the shed that housed the deep pit that served as the lavatory. He wandered down himself to inspect the place but could find nothing unusual until he noticed a piece of string sticking out under the seat. He started hauling on the string and after a couple of feet fished out the bottle of brandy which was tied to the end.

The OC also told me that in the early 1940s a Rhodesian airforce plane crash-landed not very far from where we were camped. The two young airmen started walking and came across a band of Bushmen who had just killed a giraffe. Giraffe were royal game and the Bushmen thought the airmen were policemen because they were in uniform so after pretending to befriend them they murdered them.

The police learned of this chain of events through bush gossip and arrested the leader of the band (who was called Xai pronounced Twy with a click on the first letter) and some of the senior men. However, bush gossip was not acceptable as evidence in a court of law and the police had to produce proof. Bob Langley, the trooper in charge of the investigations (who later became the Commissioner of Police) combed the area for evidence but all he could find was a piece of parachute silk and bits of uniform in the possession of the band. He told someone that he had looked down every well in the area searching for clues.

When the Bushmen were eventually tried they were acquitted because the evidence produced was too flimsy. It was quite reasonable to suppose that the airmen had started walking and had died of thirst and the jackals and hyenas had scavenged their bodies. With regard to the silk and bits of clothing found in the possession of the Bushmen this was not enough to prove they had murdered the men. So they were found not guilty.

The investigating police trooper was very downhearted and the defence attorney tried to cheer him up by saying "Never mind Bob – if at first you don't succeed you must Xai, Xai, Xai again". It was rumoured that the local chief 'dealt' with the Bushmen after they were released.

Eventually the conversation began to dwindle because it had been a long day and we prepared for bed. The OC had a wonderful overblanket – a kaross – made from the skins of black-backed jackals – the animals we had heard yelping around us. Thirty of the poor beasts had gone into its making. The two police troopers shook out their blanket rolls and settled down near the fire. Lying in my camp bed in the open and gazing up at the sky I was filled with wonder at the glory of the night sky. Many of the constellations were new to me. The Southern Cross hung over us and Orion and Scorpio glittered immensely. Lying awake I heard far away drawn-out grunting noises that were repeated several times. The OC asked if I was awake and when I replied told me they were the hunting grunts of a pride of lions that was stalking some animal nearby. Despite these wonders I was soon fast asleep and remained so until I heard movements around the campfire at dawn.

Waking up to my first African dawn in camp was a magical experience. It was deliciously cool and the thorn trees seemed to be floating above the sand that was blanketed in a light mist. The tinkling of a cow or goat bell occasionally broke the silence and the sky in the east was slowly changing colour. The police troopers were sitting on low stools near the campfire looking as though they had been there all night but one of them soon appeared at our bedsides bearing coffee in tin mugs.

After we had washed and shaved we had a tremendous bacon, egg and tomato breakfast and then struck camp and made our way back to the police post. Once again the troopers were in line to receive their OC and the inspection began. Although they looked flawless to me from where I was sitting in the shade cast by the truck I noticed that two of them got a ticking off for some deficiencies in their dress.

After the parade had been dismissed the OC and the corporal spent some time in the office. When they emerged the OC called me over and asked if I would like to accompany him on his inspection of the police quarters. These were situated in a large square piece of open ground that was edged by whitewashed stones. It was quite bare and had obviously been swept recently with brushwood. There were six rondavels each about 12 feet in diameter and beautifully kept. Behind the rondavels that were grouped in two rows of three there was a smaller hut in an enclosure that I took to be a communal kitchen. I thought it unlikely that the policemen were all bachelors but I could see no signs of any wives or companions – perhaps they had moved out for the inspection. One very good-looking young trooper had an embroidered pillow on his bed. It was skilfully done with intertwining hearts and the message was clear even though it was misspelt as 'Endles Love'.

The inspection was over by mid-morning and we set off for home. We had another pink gin, corned beef and onion lunch and got back to Francistown in the afternoon. The police captain was amused at my obvious enjoyment of the trip but I could tell he was quite flattered by it. Although I received no request from him I never told his wife about his luncheon habits in the bush.

District work

I soon began to get out into the district on my own. I didn't like trying to help run a district from an office chair. I wanted to find out what the ordinary people thought and what were the main obstacles to progress. Not being able to speak the language was a drawback but I usually managed to find a good interpreter – more often than not a schoolteacher.

The schools were a particular joy to visit. They were simple and the teaching materials were either virtually non-existent or very primitive. But the joy was in the children and usually in the teachers. Both were almost always very well dressed – the little girls in gymslips and the boys in shorts and white shirts – both usually shoeless. The teachers were nearly always immaculately turned out. Many children were taught outside under thorn trees – the luckier ones were inside in classrooms or more often the classroom since most of the schools were one-roomed affairs. But none of these drawbacks and deficiencies seemed to dampen the enthusiasm for education that was so evident. I loved to see the little girls running to school in the mornings, barefoot through the bush with a bottle of ink perched on their heads looking as though it had been fixed there by glue.

Occasionally I had to escort official visitors who were on some mission or another. They were usually terrified by anything that crawled and thought snakes and scorpions were lying in wait for them. One visitor from the World Health Organization amused me. He had a theory that the African women were reluctant to come into the maternity hospitals because when they were delivered of a child they were facing the wrong direction. I have forgotten which way he thought they preferred to be facing but I think it was in the direction of the rising sun. Another reason he advanced was that not enough care was taken in disposing of the afterbirth and if this fell into the hands of a witch doctor this gave him a powerful hold on the family.

The little Frenchman expounded these and other theories to me when we were travelling to the village he had selected for investigation – I thought he was talking nonsense but naturally kept this thought to myself. Anyway, when we arrived at the study village and assembled a bunch of women of childbearing age he set to work. He took a while to get round to his question – why did they not go to the Francistown hospital for the delivery of their babies. They discussed this at some length in their own language and then one young women stood up. She had obviously been elected as spokeswoman and she could speak good English. She said the reason why most of them stayed at home to have their children was because the fare to Francistown on Haskins' bus was five shillings return. The Frenchman was not very talkative on our return trip.

On another occasion a rather pompous man from the Colonial Office paid a visit to the station. He had no business in particular to discuss and said he was on a familiarisation tour. I could see that the District Commissioner didn't like him – or perhaps it was that he didn't trust him and suspected he was gathering material for an adverse report that would blight his future career prospects. When I suggested that I should take our visitor out for the day to let him see some administration in action the District Commissioner, glad to be rid of him, thought this was an excellent idea.

The next morning I took the visitor to a village about 20 miles from Francistown and as luck would have it the headman was presiding over a meeting of 30 or 40 village men. With permission we sat behind the headman and the interpreter and I explained to the visitor what was going on. He was very interested and at the end of the business he asked whether he could address the men. The headman was far too polite to do anything but respectfully agree and asked me to introduce him to the villagers and I did so very briefly.

Then the man from the CO addressed the gathering and to my embarrassment talked to them about agriculture – he rambled on about crop rotation that was utterly devoid of interest or relevance in a one-crop society. Anyway he enjoyed himself and I suspect he had never used an interpreter before.

At the end of his oration he wound up by saying that whilst he had enjoyed talking to them it was not for him "to teach his grandmother how to suck eggs". The interpreter who was a rather literal and not very widely read man interpreted this exactly as said. When we were preparing to leave the headman drew me aside and asked in a low voice why the visitor wanted to teach his granny how to suck eggs. I said I would tell him some other time. No doubt the old men discussed this curious ambition at length after we had left. Anyway the man from London thought he had made a hit!

Searching for a lost aircraft

Late one afternoon a police inspector came into the office. He reported that a light aircraft with three passengers on board had left for Maun (about 300 miles from Francistown) early that morning but had failed to arrive and it was feared that it had gone down somewhere in the bush. He had been told to organise search parties. The District Commissioner said he couldn't join in the search because he had to look after the station but he volunteered my services.

I didn't mind and in fact was quite looking forward to what promised to be a great adventure. However, as I pointed out, I didn't have the faintest idea where to begin searching over the three to four thousand square miles of virtually uninhabited bush much of which was covered by the Magkadikgadi salt pans that were as flat as a billiard table. The inspector said that other parties would be searching either side of the Francistown to Maun road but they wanted me to drive to Gweta (about 170 miles away on the 'main road') and then strike south west to Rakops, about 100 miles away as the crow flies. On the way from Gweta to Rakops I was to keep a look out for Bushmen or any other people and ask whether they had heard an aeroplane flying overhead and if so when they had heard it – the idea being that if they had heard the aeroplane it must have come down further to the west.

I thought it was a pretty crackpot idea but as I had no better suggestions to make I didn't comment on the method of trying to locate the crash landing. I had no difficulty about the first part of the journey. I had already visited Nata, a settlement on the way to Gweta, with my friend the OC police. But I asked about the 100 or so miles from Gweta to Rakops because as far as I knew there were no roads and not even any bush tracks so I would be driving across country. The cheerful inspector told me not to worry because he would provide a guide. This bucked me up a bit but when the guide presented himself for departure instructions and told me that he had never been to that part of the country before I began to think that we had an interesting trip ahead of us. The District Commissioner, whilst changing his spectacles before trotting off for home at the end of his day, told me to make sure I took plenty of water and petrol with me because he didn't want to organise another search party!

The 'guide' who was a cattle guard – a euphemism for a labourer in the Veterinary Department – and I set off very early the next morning and covered the first part of the journey in good time. The European storekeeper at Gweta who gave me a cup of tea but had something stronger himself, was most interested in my proposed trip. He said he didn't know of anyone who had done it before but I should be all right because the rains hadn't started and the pans would be hard and dry. When I came out of the store I saw the guide talking to an old man who was pointing out something in the distance and when I asked what the discussion was about was told the old man was pointing out the way to Rakops.

A mile or so from the store the rough sledge track petered out and we ran into very thick thorn bush and my new Chevrolet pick-up truck began its baptism of scratches. After weaving about for a while the guide said he would get on the back of the open truck so that he could point out the way better. I thought he was being a bit optimistic but I stopped and he took up his new position and guided me skilfully round the thickest of the bush until we came to the first set of pans. What a relief it was to glide along at 40mph on the hard pan surface and then I saw my first mirage. I pointed it out to the guide but he said we didn't want to go that way and pointed out the way to Rakops.

After a few miles we came to more open bush country and

began making slower but satisfactory progress. As it was getting on towards five o'clock I stopped and said we should make camp but the guide told me to keep going because there was a settlement just ahead. I was a bit puzzled but did as I was told until once more I pulled up and suggested we make camp. Again he urged me on. After about a mile I was about to stop to ask him how the hell he knew there was a settlement just ahead when he had never been in this part of the country before when, coasting over a slight rise, we came upon half a dozen huts next to a well and near a large cattle kraal. It was a cattle post owned by some faraway Motswana and staffed by Makgalagadi. I asked the guide how he had known it was there and he replied, rather scornfully I thought, that as all the cattle tracks were converging it was obvious that there was a watering point somewhere ahead.

Continuing the search to Lake Dow and Rakops

It was getting dark by the time we had set up camp near the kraals. I thought I would try the local water for an evening sundowner but I had to dispose of my drink discreetly because the water was so saline. The people in this simple little settlement didn't seem to mind our presence and went about their evening tasks. I secretly observed them with fascination. The men were delighted when a box of cigarettes was handed over and an old woman clucked with delight when my companion gave her a generous mugful of sugar.

One woman was suckling a baby and when it had sucked its fill she half turned from the firelight and held the little thing out over the sand. She then made a curious whistling/hissing noise and the baby urinated. She had some dry grass to hand and she tucked this between the little one's legs to form a nappy before wrapping it in a blanket and slinging it on her back in which position it fell fast asleep almost immediately.

Later on someone began playing a thumb piano that was constructed of tuned metal strips bound with dried animal skin cord to a small slightly concave shaped square of wood. The five flat metal strips were positioned over the slight hollow and were of diminishing lengths with the longest on the right as played. When these were flicked with the thumb they resonated in different keys. The player was very skilful and must have been entirely self-taught. The melody he produced reminded me of the sounds of cattle bells and had a strangely liquid quality. He accompanied his playing by singing a low wavering song broken now and again by soft grunts. It seemed to me that this haunting performance was describing a life of satisfying solitude but my companion thought he was singing about a hunt – perhaps we were both right.

When we turned in we were lulled to sleep by the rumbling, snuffling sounds made by cattle safely kraaled for the night. But we were awakened next morning by less romantic creatures – flies! They buzzed around so furiously that we packed up hastily and moved on to a cattle-free part of the bush where we had our breakfast. The guide told me he had broached the question of the aeroplane with the people at the cattle post but they had nothing to report so we carried on crashing occasionally through dense bush and enjoying the open stretches of flat pan country.

The pans gradually gave way to open bush. I suspected it was waterless – that is to say the water table was out of reach of the well diggers – because we saw no signs of cattle. But we saw plenty of more interesting animals – zebra, wildebeest, springbok – I gave up trying to count individual herds because they must have numbered several thousand. It was my first experience of plains game.

The guide maintained his look out position on the back of the pick-up and guided me very skilfully especially when we were in dense thorn bush. After a couple of hours or so we came to a slight ridge and the country in front of us fell away into the distance. The guide drummed softly on the roof of the truck as a signal for me to stop and said I should join him to see what was ahead. When I did I was spellbound because there in the distance was a shimmering lake – Lake Dow – full of water and pink from the many thousands of flamingos that were feeding in and fluttering above its salty waters.

My companion said there was quite a good track from Lake Dow to Rakops so we carried on in a more confident mood – or at least I did. Shortly after we sighted the lake we came across a band of Bushmen. They were fiddling about in a large thicket of bushes and I noticed they were emptying the contents of finches' nests into the skin bags they were carrying. I tried hard not to stare too obviously at them whilst my companion was talking to one of the men in a strange language but it was the first time I had seen these people although I had read a lot about them and I was totally absorbed in every detail. The little babies cradled in skin blankets on the backs of some of the women seemed happy and chubby so perhaps they fed well on nestling soup. The women carrying the babies looked too young to be mothers – they were so delicately formed and not more that five feet tall.

When we got going again I asked my companion what language he had used to converse with the man he questioned about the aeroplane and was amazed when he told me it was Fanagolo, a Zulu-based pidgin with English and Afrikaans components. He told me the Bushman had spent a few months working in the mines in South Africa and learnt some of the language then. Apparently agents of the South African Native Recruiting Corporation regularly scoured the Rakops area seeking recruits to work in the gold mines on the Witwatersrand.

We soon made it to Rakops, a small village with a trading store, police post and an office for a Stock Inspector who was not on the station at the time of our visit. The police sergeant told me he had gone to Cape Town to pick up a new wife and was expected back later that week. I learnt later that the Stock Inspector who was very deaf and in his mid-fifties had 'met' his new wife who was about his age through a lonely-hearts correspondence column in an UK newspaper. When contact was made she was living in Brighton looking after an aged mother who died soon after. Mick White – the Stock Inspector – proposed by letter. Daisy accepted and set sail for the Cape where they were married.

When I arrived in Rakops there was a stiff wind blowing and every thing was covered in thick gritty dust – it was billowing up in such clouds that the paraffin lamps had to be kept on indoors during daylight hours. This was what Mick brought Daisy to because the weather remained the same for the rest of the week. I was told that Daisy was in tears for several days after her arrival. She had lived all her life in Brighton and her trip to Africa was her first voyage overseas. She must have thought Rakops was the end of the world.

The police post was in radio contact with other stations and the sergeant came over to where I was camped shortly after we had arrived to tell me the aeroplane had been found and all was well. I learnt later that the pilot decided to treat his passengers to some game spotting from the air and after flying low for ten minutes or so couldn't spot the main road (which he had been following) when he regained height. He decided to fly roughly east knowing he would come across the wetlands of Ngamiland eventually but when he did he had run out of fuel and made a skilful landing in a clearing next to a lagoon.

So we had all been looking in the wrong place. One of the Maun residents paid a witch doctor to throw the bones and tell him where the aeroplane was which he did and described the landing place with remarkable accuracy. He had probably learnt of the forced landing through the bush telegraph but most people preferred not to accept this logical conclusion.

The pilot and three passengers suffered no ill effects. There was plenty of water and wood for a large campfire to keep the lions and elephants away. They also ate well because one of them had a .22 rifle that he used to shoot guinea fowl. But this got my District Commissioner into big trouble because he had given the man verbal permission to bring the rifle into the country when he had declared he had it during immigration formalities in Francistown. The import of .22 rifles was strictly prohibited and it was amazing that my ultra cautious District Commissioner should have acted as he did. Anyway he really got it in the neck and received a very stiff letter from headquarters. I felt sorry for him; it was probably the first time in the Service he had made an instant decision and it had blown up in his face by sheer chance.

CHAPTER 3

SOUTH TO MAHALAPYE

Looking back on my first few months in the Colonial Service most of my duties were very mundane. I had little authority and when I was not in the office dealing with unexciting paperwork I spent my time visiting the various parts of the district and writing or making verbal reports to my District Commissioner. He was very cautious and was often very uneasy about some of my recommendations especially when they in-volved spending money. There wasn't very much in the tribal treasury financial reserves but what was there was safely tucked away in some building society account. The District Commissioner once told me in reply to some criticism I made about the lack of progress that if I expected quick results I had better join the Public Works Department and build houses or something! I was outraged but there was little I could do and he ran his district much as he ran his private life I suppose. It was my bad luck to be his inexperienced and truculent assistant.

One morning after I had been on the station for about five months I was watching him painstakingly reading the incoming mail when he paused, grunted and passed a letter across saying he thought it would interest me. It most certainly did because it was an instruction from headquarters saying that as soon as could be arranged I was to take over a sub-district about 150 miles south of Francistown. The headquarters of this sub-district was a large village called Mahalapye that was on the line of rail – this was the village I had seen on a stopover on my way up to Francistown a few months earlier.

I was very excited and was all for packing my belongings and setting off south the next day but I had to contain myself because there were one or two tasks I had started and had to finish. My District Commissioner seemed to be pleased that I was being given a bit more rope. He must have been consulted about my move and reported favourably. The thought did cross my mind that he wanted to get me off his back with my irritating recommendations and criticisms but I don't think this was the case. He was a very shy man and by nature was not adventurous. Despite my truculence and irritation with the snail's pace of his methods of administration, I think he liked me and in fact had given me a good grounding in the essentials of district work. He later became a very good friend.

When I set off for Mahalapye it was pouring with rain and as we had experienced one or two very wet weeks the road was under water for long stretches. However, about ten miles or so out of Francistown it stopped raining and the sun came out. I remembered the bush as I had seen it on my way north by train a few months before and marvelled at the transformation to the lush greenness of its present state. I made good progress although the going was rather slow because of all the water that was lying about and because the road had been washed away in places but not too badly. Some way south of Francistown a very long stretch of the road was under water and I was amused to see ducks bobbing about on it.

Around midday I reached a largish village called Palapye and as this had a hotel I stopped for lunch. It was my first hotel meal in Bechuanaland and I remember it well: bean soup, pickled fish and an oxtail stew served with rice and green beans with tinned guavas to follow and rounded off with a cup of chicory coffee. I was to have many more like it in the future.

The Palapye hotel was a rather run down sort of place. I heard later that the Forestry Officer (there was only one in the entire country), who was an ex-Indian army major and a very colourful character, once spent a mosquito-plagued night there. When he went in to breakfast he pointed out to the waiter that there was no marmalade on the table. The waiter disappeared and came back to inform him that the marmalade "was finished". The major demanded to see the manager who was having his breakfast at a table in the corner. He came across and when the deficiency was pointed out to him, he said the only way he could remedy it was to get some marmalade from the trading store that adjoined the hotel because there was none in the kitchen. The major said in that case he had better do so and the persecuted manager made off. When he had returned to his cooling breakfast the waiter placed the marmalade on the table before the major. He thanked him in a loud voice and added that he didn't actually like marmalade but one couldn't breakfast properly without it being on the table – dammit!

Coupon Lou

I was interested in Palapye because it was where a celebrated *crime passionel* had been committed in the early 1940s. A wheel tapper discovered his wife *in flagrante delicto* with one of the railway clerks. Being a man of action he grabbed his .22 pistol from the bedside drawer and shot the Lothario through the heart. He was convicted of manslaughter and sentenced to a term of imprisonment in the central gaol in Gaborone. This caused problems for the gaoler because he had never had a white man in his custody before and in those days such a prisoner could not be expected to share a cell with blacks or be fed a diet of maize meal, beans and meat. But he was a resourceful man and solved his problems by giving Dunthorne (for that was the name of the cuckold) a key to his cell and arranging for him to eat at the railside hotel.

The policeman who took charge of the police post in the

village shortly after these events was a strict disciplinarian. After a busy first day taking over, he decided to pop down to the gaol and see the white prisoner because it was something of a novelty to have such a person in custody. He knew nothing of the gaoler's rather novel arrangements and was alarmed when he found the cell empty. He routed out the gaoler and when the position was explained bawled him out and set off for the hotel where he thought the prisoner might still be. When he got there he was told that Mr Dunthorne had finished his dinner about an hour ago. He asked around and was told that he might then have gone on to visit 'Coupon Lou'.

This was the sobriquet of the wife of a government driller. She was often alone at home whilst her husband was far out in the bush drilling for water. She had earned her name during the war when she used to dish out favours to men in return for coupons then found in packets of cigarettes and which could be exchanged for various goods. Apparently she was still in business – but not for coupons – and had taken a shine to Dunthorne or perhaps being a kindly soul just felt sorry for him.

The policeman repaired to her bungalow and she answered his hammering on the door by appearing in a nightgown, rather heavily but inexpertly made up and smoking a cigarette in a long holder. She denied that the prisoner was there and with absolutely no authority he insisted on searching her house. The policeman was particularly interested in the bedroom. He looked in the wardrobe and under the bed with no result. He was standing pondering his next move with Coupon Lou standing at his elbow when he saw the mattress rise slightly then fall. He looked under the bed again but this time more carefully and saw the naked Dunthorne hanging on to the springs with his toes and fingers. He hauled him out and Coupon Lou feigning amazement, exclaimed "Mr Dunthorne what are you doing in my bedroom?"

Introduction to Mahalapye

I arrived in Mahalapye in the late afternoon and decided to book into the hotel for the night and sort out my bits and pieces the next day. I showered and was changing into fresh clothes when there was a loud knocking on the door of the rondavel that was my hotel room – it was the police Station Commander who said he needed to see me. I opened the door and was greeted with a very smart salute by the sub-inspector who looked even younger than I was. He told me he had arrested a European for assaulting an African and as he had no place to hold him whilst awaiting trial he wondered if I could hear the case that afternoon. What he meant of course was that it was unthinkable to put a white man in a blacks only gaol.

He drove me to my office which was tiny but which was also used as the courtroom. I got myself settled behind the desk and he wheeled in the accused, one Billy Biemont who was a Hollander by birth and farmed in a European farming block about 30 miles from Mahalapye. He was a fair-haired, stocky man of about thirty dressed in khaki shirt and shorts with a deep sunburn that emphasised the bright blue of his eyes. He looked a bit the worse for wear and had a bruised cheek. I guessed he had been drinking. He pleaded not guilty when the charge was read out and said the African had assaulted him. So the sub-inspector proceeded with the prosecution case.

After both parties had presented their version of what had happened the facts were quite clear. When the accused left the bar which opened on to the railway station platform to visit the lavatory he stumbled into the complainant who was mending a puncture and had the bicycle inner tube immersed in a bucket of water. In the stumble some of water was spilt. The complainant shouted at the accused who picked up the bucket and rammed it on the complainant's head. The latter replied by lashing out at him with his fists and the accused responded in similar fashion.

I asked the accused what he would do if he were mending a puncture and someone trampled over him and in response to his protests rammed a half full bucket of water over his head. He replied that he "would donner him" which I gathered was Afrikaans (and probably Dutch) for he "would thump him". So I fined the accused £10 or one month in gaol. He paid up and left on his motor bike in the direction of the hotel.

The Sub-inspector told me that Billy Biemont was a hard working and very successful farmer. He grew onions and flowers under irrigation and was able to sell them on the Johannesburg market early in the season at very good prices. His motorbike was very useful for riding up and down his irrigation ditches when tending his crops. But he was a bit like a bull terrier and needed a scrap from time to time.

Once when he was thirsting for action he jumped on his motor bike and called on a neighbouring farmer who had the reputation of having been a very good fighter in his day. Billy explained what he wanted. Rhodes Brink, his neighbour, said he couldn't oblige him because he had recently developed heart trouble but he knew of a man over in the Transvaal at a village called Vaalwater who was said to be very good with his fists and perhaps he would oblige. His offer of a letter of introduction was eagerly accepted and he wrote formally using the salutation "Waarde Heer" (Esteemed Sir). Armed with this letter Billy roared off on his bike into the late afternoon bound for Vaalwater on the other side of the Limpopo.

When he arrived the village was virtually deserted and a young lad told him most of the people were at the hotel where they were having a melon feast and a dance. Billy repaired to the hotel and asked the barman if the addressee of his letter was around and was told he was dancing. He asked the barman to give him the letter. Billy was having a beer when a huge Afrikaner came in holding the opened letter and in a loud voice asked "Waar is Biemont?" Billy chirped up and his adversary, looking down on him, warned him that he was a very good fighter to which Billy replied that was what he was looking for. So they set to out in the yard and after the Goliath had floored Billy several times they retired to the bar and got roaring drunk together. Having spent the night drinking with his adversary, Billy returned to his farm the next morning on his motor bike hungover and bruised but happy. I was most impressed by this tale and looked forward to seeing more of this strange fellow.

I returned to the hotel and decided to have a drink at the bar. This was the bar with the lion's head on the wall that had caught my attention on my way through several months earlier. There were a dozen or more people at the counter so the bar was pretty full. There was a rather awkward silence when I came in but the locals readily made space for me. I ordered a beer and when I offered the money to pay for it the friendly barman said it had been paid for and jerked his head towards the end of the bar. Billy Biemont raised his glass and gave me a broad grin accompanied by a wink.

Seretse Khama and the chieftainship dispute

My sub-district was part of the large territory of the Bamangwato tribe – one of the principal tribes of Bechuanaland. Apart from Mahalapye, it had four other large centres of population – large that is for a sparsely populated country like Bechuananland. All of these villages had populations of around 5,000 each and there were numerous other smaller villages. Each of the larger villages was in charge of a Subordinate African authority. These men were subordinate to the African Authority who lived in the tribal headquarters in Serowe that was about 100 miles from Mahalapye.

The African Authority was a statutory appointment because at that time the tribe did not have a traditional chief. The heir to the chieftainship was Seretse Khama. His father, Sekgoma Khama died in 1925 when Seretse was a young child so the boy's uncle Tshekedi Khama was summoned from his studies at Fort Hare College in South Africa to act as Regent. Seretse was sent to school and university in South Africa by his uncle and in 1945 he went up to Oxford and took up residence at Balliol College. In 1946 he left Oxford and registered for studies at the Inns of Court (Inner Temple) in London. In 1947 he met Ruth Williams a 24-year-old white woman at a YMCA dance. He fell in love with her and a year later without seeking permission from his uncle Tshekedi and the tribal elders he married her in London at the Kensington Registry Office.

A fierce tribal dispute followed. Seretse was adamant that he proposed to stick by the woman of his choice whom he loved deeply. Tshekedi and the royal uncles were furious and made it clear that if Seretse did not drop his wife he could not become chief. At first it looked as though the traditionalists led by Tshekedi would win the day but powerful interventions by Seretse at tribal gatherings persuaded the younger elements in the tribe to accept him as chief and Ruth as his wife.

However this was not to be. In 1948 the Nationalist Party in South Africa ousted the United Party by gaining a landslide victory in a general election. A cornerstone of National Party policy was the separation of races in South Africa by its apartheid policy which it described rather curiously as a separate but equal form of government. The very idea of a mixed marriage of an important person in a neighbouring state was repugnant to the Nationalists more particularly as they still entertained notions of taking over Bechuanaland and turning it into a black enclave of the Union of South Africa. It is almost certain that the South African government brought diplomatic pressure to bear on the Labour government in the UK through the British High Commissioner in South Africa. The shameful outcome was that in August 1950 Seretse Khama accompanied by his wife and baby daughter flew out of Bechuanland into exile in the UK.

What should have been obvious to all concerned in this shoddy episode in British colonial history was that the Bamang-wato revered Seretse Khama and a majority of them wanted him as their chief. However, leading tribesmen who remained vocif-erously loyal to Seretse were regarded with deep suspicion by the administration and they figured largely in the various intelligence reports that landed on our desks. Some of these reports had stamped on each page in deep red the words "UK Eyes Only". I thought this was very curious seeing that many of the senior officials who compiled and read them had been born in South Africa. However, I was far too junior to get involved in high politics and I had a job of work to do.

Meeting the Rutherfords

I soon got myself settled in my house in Mahalapye. Our houses were quite generously provided with basic furniture and as yet I hadn't acquired many possessions. My monthly salary after deductions for rent, vehicle purchase etc was £23 but it went a long way. I had three servants and was able to afford a rifle and a refrigerator. In those days refrigerators were standard issue only on remote stations, Maun, Tshabong and Ghanzi for in-stance.

I spent a couple of days reading the files and getting to know the officials on the station and other people in the village. Then

I received a radio message from Bruce Rutherford who was the District Commissioner and my superior officer, inviting me to spend a long weekend with him at Serowe the district as well as the tribal headquarters. We had never met and I was looking forward to meeting him because I had heard good reports about him.

When I arrived at his office he gave me a generous welcome and told me he had asked me to come over so we could get to know each other. He was a big bear of a man in his late forties. He had come up through the ranks, having started off life in the service as a magistrate's clerk. The Seretse Khama business had made the Serowe posting a very difficult one and I suppose he had been chosen specially for it. I knew immediately that I was going to enjoy working under him.

He was completely unflappable and had a delightful sense of humour. In his quiet and unassuming way he was also very brave. When one of his young District Officers contracted polio, arrangements were made to transfer him by air to a hospital in Johannesburg. A small five-seater plane duly arrived at the landing strip and it was necessary to transfer the desperately ill patient to it. Polio is infectious and the hospital staff seemed a bit reluctant to get too close. Bruce gathered up the stricken fellow in his arms, put him on the back seat of his car and transferred him to the aeroplane.

At the end of the morning he took me up to the Residency to meet his wife. She was Scottish and a real burrah memsahib. I believe wives of junior officials were expected to call on her wearing hat and gloves when they first arrived on the station and at intervals thereafter and they failed to do so at their peril. I could see that she was a formidable woman but she was a most gracious hostess. Her garden was absolutely magnificent. She had inherited it from previous marvellous gardeners but the green lawns edged with beds of cannas and the magnificent bougainvillea-draped thorn trees and walls were a credit to her. As I was to discover she was also a splendid cook. I took to her at once and was gratified that she seemed to take an immediate liking to me. She was very outspoken but I liked that because you always knew where you were with her.

Although my bachelor establishment in Mahalapye was comfortable enough it was a bit sparse so it was delightful to spend a few days with the Rutherfords in their gracious home enjoying their generous hospitality. Chatting with my hosts that first evening they told me that the house had a bad reputation. Although they had not heard or seen anything untoward it was said to be haunted by a poltergeist because it had been built on the site of an ancient burial ground. One previous occupant was adamant that he had seen a Bushman standing on the back verandah staring out into the night. Another previous occupant who was a bachelor refused to stay in the house after several disturbed nights and moved out to one of the other houses. I wasn't much of a ghost man and thought the tales about the house interesting but unlikely to be true.

Later I was shown to my bedroom that opened out onto the 'Bushman verandah'. The old house was full of shadows because after the domestic generator had been switched off for the night oil lamps and candles were the only means of illumination. It was a large house with a tin roof – the usual roof construction material in those days. When the tin was cooling down after the heat of the day it creaked and groaned and this went on into the night.

I was soon tucked up in bed reading by candlelight when I heard a strange noise – a low moaning accompanied by a muffled hollow tapping. I lay in bed uneasily whilst the noise was repeated three or four times. At last I got up and peered out through the French doors onto the moonlit verandah but I couldn't see any signs of the ghostly Bushman. I was about to return to bed when I heard the noise again. It was coming from the wardrobe and when I opened the doors the house cat emerged looking rather resentful and stalked through the French doors with its tail held high in the air. The Rutherfords enjoyed my account of the haunting over breakfast the next day.

The evening before I was due to return to Mahalapye, the District Commissioner said he wanted to have a private chat with me and we went out on to the lawn with our drinks. He told me he was short staffed and would not be able to visit me very often as there was much to attend to at tribal headquarters because of 'the troubles' associated with the chieftainship. He asked me to report to him about once a month in person to keep him fully in the picture. He said that he was also gazetted as District Commissioner of the Tuli Block which adjoined the Bamangwato District and he saw no hope of visiting that either so he asked me whether I would help him by supervising it as well as looking after my sub-district. I was flattered and delighted and agreed readily.

I was very fortunate because the southern part of the Bamangwato Tribal Territory and the Tuli Block were quite different both in natural features and in their administrative requirements. In the tribal area the concerns of the tribesmen centred around schooling for their children, medical facilities, water supplies and the prices received for their cattle in the local trading stores and of course the chieftainship issue caused much dissatisfaction. In the Tuli Block most of the farmers were Afrikaans. Most of them belonged to the Nationalist Party and regarded South Africa as their homeland. They resented the alien flag and the British administration and its officials.

Tshekedi Khama

In each of the four principal villages in the Bamangwato part of my district there was a Subordinate African Authority – subordinate that is to the African Authority in Serowe who had been appointed by the government to assume the responsibilities of chieftainship. These subordinate authorities were all men in their early fifties and were fine examples of the Bamangwato ruling class. They had served under Tshekedi Khama, Seretse's uncle, who had ruled the tribe as Regent since 1925, when Seretse's father had died. Seretse was then four years old. Tshekedi was very autocratic and ruled the tribe with a rod of iron but he had a first class mind – far superior to many set up in authority over him. He had established a very efficient administration and the Subordinate African Authorities I had to deal with were his disciples.

When the chieftainship issue was at its height in 1949 it became apparent after several stormy tribal meetings that support was seeping away from Tshekedi so he decided to go into voluntary exile with 43 of his followers in the neighbouring territory of the Bakwena tribe. They settled in a village called Rametsana that was just over the tribal boundary.

A few years later Tshekedi returned to the Bamangwato Tribal Territory and settled in a village called Pilikwe that was about 50 miles from Serowe and on the east of the railway line. It was just outside my sub-district but frequently, when central government wanted messages passed to Tshekedi, I was required to be the messenger (in those days there were few telephones in the Territory and none in Pilikwe) so I got to know him fairly well.

He was a most impressive man and under his iron rule Pilikwe was a model village. He lived in a European type bungalow himself but nearly all the other dwellings were traditional Batswana round huts with thatched roofs and surrounded by courtyards. The thatching was immaculate and untended sheep and goats were not tolerated in the village. There was not a scrap of litter to be seen. Whenever I went to see him we usually ended up in his study and I never failed to be impressed by his library – it would have done credit to any Cambridge don. I couldn't help feeling that he was very familiar with the content of most of the books that lined the walls. I often thought it very sad that it had not been possible to keep him on board and that he was allowed to vegetate in his model village

The first time I visited him we were sitting on the verandah having tea when one of his female domestics brought a message to him. She approached bending so low that she was almost on her knees and after he had received the message she retreated in similar fashion. I was very green then and asked him if the woman was disabled. He seemed puzzled and when I explained that her stooping posture had led me to conclude that she was deformed he was most amused at my ignorance and said his servants usually approached him in this way. Whenever we had occasion to walk through the village I noticed how deferentially he was treated. Nobody ever walked past him without acknowledging his presence. The villagers stopped and bowed and greeted him with a gentle soundless clapping of their hands. He always acknowledged these greetings.

It was Tshekedi who caused a diplomatic incident in September 1933 when he allegedly had a white man called Phineas McIntosh flogged in his kgotla. Admiral Evans was the acting High Commissioner and was stationed in Cape Town. Colonel Rey was the Resident Commissioner stationed in Mafikeng. They both regarded this alleged flogging as an affront to white colonial power and prestige and together they conspired to teach this 'uppity native' a lesson. Evans sent a detachment of marines to arrest Tshekedi in his land-locked fortress after which he would be banished from his tribal territory. The marines' gun carriages got bogged down in the sand and the story was often related that Tshekedi obligingly sent teams of oxen to pull them out. If he did he must have enjoyed the farce hugely. He was then arrested and briefly banished but he was re-instated a few weeks later after a public outcry in Britain.

I got to know Phineas McIntosh fairly well. When I was stationed in Mahalapye he was a government driller prospecting for coal in my sub district and I visited his camp from time to time. He told me what happened.

Having lived in Serowe for most of his life he regarded himself as a tribesman. He was a blacksmith by trade and together with a companion (Henry McNamee) had made a habit of whoring and fighting in the village after heavy drinking bouts. Tshekedi frequently complained about them to the District Commissioner who, being rather weak, did nothing. Getting no action from the District Commissioner Tshekedi sent his tribal police to bring the young tearaways to the kgotla (the traditional meeting place where tribal affairs were discussed and disputes settled). When Tshekedi approached his stool in the kgotla, Phineas, who regarded him as his chief, prostrated himself. Seeing Phineas throwing himself forward, the tribal police thought he was about to attack Tshekedi and they roughed him up.

Phineas assured me that this is what happened. He said he bore no resentment to Tshekedi who had not ordered him to be flogged, that he had been behaving badly and expected to be 'dealt with'. Phineas was a grand old timer. To see this gentle man over 20 years after the event with his wife Margaret and his son and daughter, it was difficult to believe that he had been so wild and had caused a detachment of marines to be bogged down in the sand outside Serowe. I never asked Tshekedi for his version of these events – I think I was in such awe of him that I would never have dared question him about such personal happenings.

District work and pleasure

The Subordinate African Authorities in my district must have regarded me almost as a schoolboy but nevertheless they treated me with profound courtesy and respect and I responded in a similar fashion. It seemed to me that they were more than capable of running their own affairs and I soon learned not to interfere unless it seemed necessary which was rarely. I was their link with central government and when they needed guidance they asked for it. I was flattered when they turned to me for help – for instance to replace an unsatisfactory teacher, to get agricultural extension workers allocated to their area, to persuade the Public Works Department to provide equipment to scrape a road or drill a borehole or simply to ask my advice on some matter that was troubling them.

Mahalapye wasn't much to look at. It was untidy and sprawling and usually devoid of vegetation. When the wind blew it whipped up huge clouds of dust but I loved the place and was very happy there. I got on very well with the Subordinate African Authority there – Gasebalwe Seretse – who was one of Seretse Khama's uncles. He was very light skinned and had almost oriental eyes. He had been a schoolteacher and spoke very good English but he always addressed me through an interpreter. Perhaps he was hinting that I should learn to address him in Setswana. He invariably carried a slim copper rod about 18 inches long and when talking would polish it with his spare hand.

One Monday morning he came to my office and reported that

the senior children from the local school had visited a school about 50 miles away over the weekend for a sports function. Some of the boys had got drunk and indecently assaulted several of the girls and a couple of the female teachers. He had consulted the parents and with their agreement proposed to haul before the kgotla all those who went on the trip, sort out the culprits and give them six of the best. He said he thought he should let me know in advance because he knew the administration was sensitive about corporal punishment. I told him I thought he was proposing to do exactly what I would do if I were in his place so off he went and gave the young thugs what they deserved.

About a month later I got a very worried radio message from my District Commissioner – Bruce Rutherford – informing me that a question had been put down for answer in the House of Commons by Fenner Brockway about schoolchildren being flogged at Mahalapye in Bechuanaland. This British MP used to be fed information by a disgruntled supporter of Seretse Khama who was always looking for an opportunity to discredit the administration – this supporter had been imprisoned by the British during the tribal troubles so I suppose he had little reason to love us. But he had got this one wrong. The 'schoolchildren' were 16 and 17 year olds who when violently drunk had indecently assaulted females on the school trip. They deserved what they got and when I explained what had actually happened I heard no more about it. Gasebalwe Seretse was amused when I told him he had achieved fame in the British House of Commons but I could tell he was grateful that I had supported him.

Shoshong was another principal settlement in my district. The Subordinate African Authority there – Sethogile Kgamane – was another of Seretse's uncles. He was a grand fellow with an impressive air of authority and a very able administrator. The village was about 20 miles west of Mahalapye and nestled snuggly against very attractive hills. It was spread around the mouth of a gorge in these hills and except in the depth of the dry season there was usually a little stream trickling out of it. At one time it was the tribal capital but Seretse Khama's grandfather moved his people to another site when water became a problem. The settlement was originally established around the foothills partly because there was water nearby but also because when the village was attacked – usually by the Matabele – the people could take refuge amongst the rocky outcrops in the gorge and elsewhere.

Shoshong was an early centre of missionary activity. David Livingstone must have known it well and the Price family, in-laws of the Moffats (who were also Livingstone's in laws) lived there for several years. An old man showed me a large square boulder which when struck with a big stone rang as clearly and loudly as a bell. He told me the missionaries used it to summon the people to church – his grandfather probably told him about this.

One of the traders told me an amusing story about Shoshong in the late 1880s. Apparently a German entomologist visited the area to collect specimens and amassed a sizeable collection of spiders, scorpions, snakes etc that he preserved in bottles containing surgical spirit. He wanted to go on further up country to continue collecting and he arranged to leave his collection with one of the traders for safekeeping. Little did he know.

The supply wagon from the south had been held up for some reason and the two traders on the station ran out of liquor. The one who was looking after the specimens told the other that the jars he had contained liquor as well as the scorpions etc and suggested that they sample some. However, the other trader expressed fears about being poisoned. Whilst they were wondering what to do they saw dust rising down the valley and soon an itinerant trader pulled up outside the store where the specimens were stored. He received a warm welcome and was given a generous drink decanted from one of the jars. The thirsty traders watched him for some time and when he appeared to suffer no ill effects they shooed him away and had one hell of a party. What the German said when he came to collect his specimens was not recorded.

Beyond the Shoshong hills the country was sandveldt and became drier and drier as it reached out to the Kalahari Desert. It was good cattle country when very deep boreholes could provide water but for the most part it was waterless and home to vast herds of wildebeest, springbok and eland. I spent many weekends after visits to Shoshong camped in this marvellous wilderness shooting the odd wildebeest or springbok when it was the open season – eland were royal game and protected – or otherwise simply enjoying the loneliness and at night listening to the lions and jackals from the safety of a huge camp fire. The skies at night with their glittering southern constellations were glorious.

Another favourite spot of mine was a place called Lephepe about 30 miles south west of Shoshong. There was no proper village there but there was a large pan that usually held water throughout the season. The duck shooting was splendid. There was quite a concentration of cattle because of the water but they roamed far away from the pan having grazed flat most of the nearby surrounding area. I would camp well away from this overgrazed area and enjoyed many evenings listening to the hunting grunts of lions which abounded in the bush around the pan because of the ready supply of cattle. I was told that Seretse Khama's father – Sekgoma – after a dispute with his father was exiled to Lephepe. I thought at the time it was the sort of fate I would much enjoy.

On one of these camping trips I had a conversation with my general servant Sebogile and the government messenger about African nicknames for Europeans they knew. I had heard that these could be devastatingly accurate. They told me that one of the Mahalapye traders was generally known amongst the Africans as 'the man with sores under his armpits'. It took me a while to get the English version of the nickname out of them but when I did its cruel accuracy was immediately apparent because he walked with both elbows held high in the air. Another resident was called 'leeba' (the dove) because he was a gentle man who rarely raised his voice. Yet another was called 'phokobje' (the jackal) because of his curious high pitched laugh. A woman was referred to as 'Mma cardbox' because she had once displayed a notice fashioned out of a cardboard box saying that she did not require any servants. Some of the locals were puzzled that Dennis Atkins was not related to George Atkinson.

However, they were very wary when I asked them for my nickname. After much persuasion they told me I was known at first as 'Araba potso' which means 'Answer the question' because I frequently used this expression when presiding in court. This was when I was learning the ropes and before I realised that most witnesses preferred to give their version of events in their own way which was not always the most direct. But after a while this nickname was replaced by 'Segata borokwe' which is the one that stuck. It means 'He who walks on his trousers' – in those days my slim hips didn't support my trousers very well and my turn-ups hung low about my shoes and sometimes scraped the ground.

Around the bar at the Mahalapye Hotel

When I wasn't absent from the station on tour I used to visit the Mahalapye hotel several times a week for a few beers, games of liar dice with matches as 'stake money' and always a chat. It was more like a social club for whites than a public bar. In those days Africans were excluded because of the liquor laws. When three of their principal chiefs journeyed to England in 1895 to beg Queen Victoria to prevent their tribal areas being ceded to Cecil Rhodes and the British South Africa Company – which she did – they also asked her to keep white man's liquor away from their people.

The bar humour was often rough and earthy. When a woman from the mail train dragged her husband into the bar and enjoined him to look at the lion's head on the wall, one of the locals piped up that it was nothing and he "should see its arse in the dining room".

I was told that on one occasion a plot was hatched to put some haughty woman on the station in her place – I think she was the doctor's wife. Apparently she had condemned the bar as a den of vice and had said uncomplimentary things about some of the clientele. The barman's wife sent the lady's name off to several magazines which advertised various services – help with passing the Standard VI examination, how to reduce piles without surgery, the removal of corns, how to get rid of dandruff and a sure fire cure for constipation. The poor woman was deluged with unwanted literature.

One night in the bar when we were without a doctor on the station the Veterinary Officer told us about one of his miraculous cures. When he returned from tour the previous evening his wife told him that the Livestock Officer who was their neighbour was very ill. After supper the vet went around to find out what the trouble was and found two of the station wives attending to the patient with wet towels, ice and sympathy. When the vet asked the sick man what the trouble was he said he hadn't passed water for several days. Although the two women protested that they had trained as nurses and knew what they were doing, the vet ordered them from the room but told them first to bring him a bucket and a salt cellar that poured. He readied the patient by getting him to sit on the edge of the bed, told him the cure would sting but he guaranteed it would work and wrapping his hand round his penis poured salt down the urethra and held the bucket at the ready. The treatment worked like magic and the patient leant back much relieved. The vet told us that when racehorses are transferred to a new stable they sometimes suffer from urine retention and the salt business was standard treatment. He added that when people were sick from the waist up a doctor was their best bet but from the waist down a vet always knew the most effective remedy.

The bar crowd was vastly amused one evening when an event of that afternoon was described. One of the houses had been standing empty for a month or so. A Public Works Department road foreman on transfer to the station had been told that it was to be his house. He was approaching Mahalapye having been on the road for a couple of hours or more when his enormously fat wife said she needed to pee. He declined to stop there and then because he said they were nearly at their house with the result that when they arrived the fat lady was bursting.

She scrambled out of the truck, scuttled round to the back where the outside lavatory was located complete with a bucket removable through a trap door in the back and plonked her vast backside on the seat. She was in full flow when she leapt in the air screaming that a snake had bitten her on the behind. Her puny husband inspected her huge bottom, saw the two red prong marks and bundling her into the truck drove furiously to the dispensary in the village where an African orderly pumped some snake bite serum into her. The husband took his fainting wife home and got her on to a bed then went to inspect the latrine armed with his shot gun. He nudged the door open with the barrel and peered cautiously inside. Nothing was stirring so he edged forward and again with the barrel slowly lifted the lavatory seat. Still nothing so he inched forward and when he peered in he saw a rather wet broody hen looking angrily up at him.

The Tuli Block

The other part of my district – the Tuli Block – bordered the Crocodile/Limpopo River and with one exception all the farms were owned by whites. The area was originally part of the Bamangwato Tribal Territory and was ceded by Khama III (Seretse's grandfather) who was the chief of the Bamangwato at the time to the British South Africa Company in 1895 for the purpose of the construction of a railway by that company. Khama readily agreed to cede this strip of land because he wanted a buffer between his people and the Transvaal Boers. It was ironic that 60 years later over 90 per cent of the farms in this erstwhile buffer strip were owned by Transvaal Afrikaners.

The Tuli Block had its own headquarters at Machaneng. There were government offices there as well as a Residency for the District Commissioner and bungalows for the Stock Inspector, the OC Police and his two sub-inspectors. There were also 'lines' for the police corporal and constables and for the clerks. There was a gaol and a parade ground edged with white-washed stones and always kept neatly swept. On one side of the parade ground facing the court house was a row of syringa trees. On hot days when these were in flower their scent which swept into the courtroom was almost overpowering. In the far north, near the boundary with Southern Rhodesia, the Baines Drift police post was manned by a white sub-inspector and half a dozen constables.

The Block was about ten miles deep and 200 miles long. It

was typical bushveldt country and spectacularly beautiful particularly in the north near the Tuli Circle. It was separated from the Transvaal by the Crocodile River that further downstream became known as the Limpopo. I was fascinated to see that it was grey-green and greasy and was "all set about with fever trees".

The northern farms bounded in the south by the Macloutsie River were mostly hunting blocks with absentee owners. They were teeming with game – elephant, lion, eland, kudu, leopard, impala, hyena, wild dog, jackals, guinea fowl and the rivers abounded with fish. I heard lions giving their hunting grunt whenever I camped there and jackals and hyenas were usually in full voice. In the middle and south of the Block there was less game although it was still fairly plentiful and the landowners there were usually resident and went in for serious farming. There was always quite a lot of poaching going on and also much smuggling of cattle when prices were higher in South Africa than they were in Bechuanaland, as they usually were. I believe most of the farmers had brands registered in Bechuanaland with the numbers widely spaced so when they got the cattle across the border they simply filled in the space with another number to create a South African registered brand.

Most of the farmers were Afrikaners. I'm afraid there was much racial tension because most of the Bechuanaland police, both black and white, viewed them with deep suspicion. This was partly because of their nationality and also because they thought they were either actual or potential poachers or smugglers or both. In many cases this was absolutely correct. For the most part I liked them very much. They were very hospitable and although at first they were suspicious of the English magistrate they were soon won round. Some of them spoke very little English but somehow we managed.

Once an over zealous police sub-inspector – an English speaking South African – took a £10 on the spot fine from one of the farmers because when he searched his truck under some flimsy pretext, he found two bottles of brandy on the front seat and the farmer did not have a removal permit. Legally, such a permit was needed to remove purchased liquor from licensed premises (principally to try and prevent unscrupulous people from illegally selling liquor to 'natives') but few people took any notice of this obscure provision of the liquor laws. I was appalled because I realised the police sub-inspector had acted out of sheer malice and in those days £10 was a hefty sum. I gave the sub-inspector an earful and refused to confirm the fine. The farmer was certainly guilty so I directed the policeman to bring him to court. About two weeks later he appeared before me looking terribly nervous – he probably thought he would go to gaol. I found him guilty as charged but let him off with a warning. Someone told me that later outside the court he remarked to one of his friends that he never thought an 'Engelsman' could be so fair to an Afrikaner.

The man I had met in Mahalapye on my first afternoon there – Billy Biemont – farmed in the Tuli Block and we became good friends. I often spent the night with him in his rambling and ramshackle farmhouse. He was very hospitable and usually drank far too much when he had a drinking companion. We slept on the back verandah because it was airy and cool. Billy often alarmed me by trying to shoot bats with his .303 whilst lying in bed. It was obviously impossible to wing a bat in this way – apart from their speed the only light was from paraffin lamps so the ceiling space was in almost total darkness. I believe that Billy had to patch the bullet holes in his roof before the rainy season to keep his verandah dry.

The owner of an hotel in the Tuli Block told me that one afternoon there were several farmers drinking in the bar when

Billy rolled in – barrel-chested and sunburnt and wearing very short shorts. He ordered a beer. It was obvious that he was looking for some action. Billy settled down and the farmers carried on chatting in Afrikaans. They were talking about food and one of them said that pumpkins were his favourite vegetables. Billy scornfully and aggressively remarked to no one in particular that in Holland they fed pumpkins to the pigs. A shouting match followed which developed into a bar brawl and, being heavily outnumbered Billy was thrashed and thrown out. When order was restored and the drinkers had settled down again the pumpkin-loving farmer told the landlord that much as he hated the Rooineks (the English) he hated the Kaaskops (Hollanders) more!

Fortunately it was necessary for me to visit the northern Tuli Block fairly regularly. I had to liaise quite closely with the sub-inspector in charge of the Baines Drift police post who was concerned principally with the poaching and cattle rustling which was almost a way of life in the area. There was also quite a bit of other crime – stock theft, assaults, non-payment of tax etc. – so I was kept quite busy on my visits. In the police store there was a set of stocks that must have been there for many years. Once when the Resident Commissioner (who, in effect, was the Governor of the territory) visited the station he noticed these stocks. He was very interested in what he regarded as a relic of the old days and remarked to me that it must have been very many years since they were used. I mumbled a non-committal reply because I knew that the sub-inspector had used them the previous month to restrain a particularly vicious man whom he had arrested for a serious assault – the lock-up facilities at Baines Drift were almost totally insecure.

Bob Maskell, the sub-inspector, was a very good policeman – nothing flustered him. He was slightly older than I was. He had served in the army and he managed his little police detachment with great authority. Once during the rainy season I was due to go to Baines Drift to hold court but before I set off I received a radio message informing me that the Limpopo was in flood and the police post, which was on a slight hillock, was surrounded by water. The radio message also stated that food supplies were very low. I raised Bob on the radio and we had a two-way conversation. I asked him what the situation was with the dozen or so waiting trial prisoners if the food supply was low. In his unflappable, matter-of-fact voice he informed me that he had told the prisoners to 'bugger off' and come back when the floods had subsided. He had and they did!

Bob used to come into Mahalapye periodically because this was civilisation to him and he could stock up with supplies there. I suppose it would have been easier for him to go across to the Northern Transvaal via one of the many drifts across the Limpopo but he didn't much like the Afrikaners in that part of the world. He was popular in the Mahalapye bar. One night we were talking about smuggling in the Tuli Block and he told us that when he was in the army in the Middle East, he had to deal with quite a bit of smuggling – mainly gold and diamonds. He said a favourite trick employed by the smugglers was to conceal the smuggled item in a condom and secrete it up their backsides. The barmaid expressed her surprise and thought it must have been terribly painful. Bob rounded on her and scornfully asked her if she had never seen "an Arab's arsehole".

On one of my trips to Baines Drift the road on the Bechuana-land side was in poor condition following heavy rains so I went up on the Transvaal side intending to cross at the oddly named Zanzibar Drift. Just before the crossing there was a trading store and I decided to call in and stretch my legs. The store-keeper was very hospitable. He apologised for his poor English but I said it was much better than my Afrikaans and this seemed to please him. He offered me tea and I accepted. I think that before I arrived he had been drinking something stronger than tea even though it was mid morning. The tea was produced on a tray and we were standing at the counter drinking it when his young wife appeared no doubt to see the Englishman – in those days quite a rarity in that part of the world. Her English was very poor. She was toting a baby boy who was the image of his storekeeper father. I remarked on this and she agreed. She said he was a "blick off the old chop".

Whilst I was drinking my tea the storekeeper was chatting away, his tongue probably loosened by whatever liquor he had been drinking. When I said that there didn't seem to be many potential customers living near the store he winked and said he did quite well out of various things – hides, skins, dagga (marijuana) and other commodities – that were smuggled across from Bechuanaland.

When I had finished drinking my tea he offered me more but I said I had to go because I was expected in Baines Drift where I had to preside in court. He cried out "God, die bloody magistraat". I said my farewells and left. A couple of days later on my way back from Baines Drift I called in at the South African police post at Alldays and asked the sergeant about the storekeeper at Zanzibar. He smiled and produced a fat file marked with his name. The sergeant said he had been trying to pin something on him for a year or more but he was as slippery as an eel. I decided it wasn't necessary to tell the sergeant what I had been told over morning tea and went on my way.

Preparing for Seretse's return

Having to divide my time between the Mahalapye district and the Tuli Block was not in the least burdensome and I didn't mind spending most of my time on tour. I loved the bushveldt and the driver, messenger/interpreter and cook who formed the camping team were wonderful companions.

In late September 1956 I returned from a trip to find one of those 'Top Secret for UK eyes only' letters waiting for me. It had been delivered to the police inspector by special courier and he had locked it up in his safe. I was intrigued but when I opened it and read it I could hardly believe the good news it contained. The British Government had agreed that Seretse Khama could return home. I told the police inspector in confidence what was afoot. He was uneasy. He said Seretse and his supporters were bound to be bitter about the exile and would cause trouble. I thought he was mistaken but said we could only wait and see.

I was instructed to make the announcement in the main villages in my sub district all on the same day and as close together time wise as possible. This was a tall order because the villages were fair distances apart. There was also a big parcel containing copies of the announcement I had to make. The idea was to make the announcement and leave copious supplies of it in written form so the tribesmen could digest what I had said. I thought this a pretty daft arrangement because even though the printed copies had been translated into Setswana, only a small proportion of the tribesmen were literate. I would much rather have told the tribesmen in my own words what was going to happen but I had to do as instructed.

The next morning I set off early and visited each of the principal villages to tell the Subordinate African Authorities I would be returning the next day and gave them a time and asked them to summon their people because I had to make a very important announcement. Because of the distance between the villages I could only visit the last one – a village called Sefhare – in the middle of the afternoon. My old friend Gasebalwe Seretse was the Subordinate African Authority having been transferred there from Mahalapye a short while before. When I told him I intended to address a meeting in his village in the afternoon he was aghast and, speaking English for once, told me that as I well knew that was the worst possible time to hold a meeting because most of the villagers would be drunk. I said I was acting under orders and had no choice.

Rather to my surprise the first three meetings went well and there was no trouble but I was not looking forward to visiting Sefhare. The announcement had not been well drafted and went into too much detail about the reasons for the banishment and the need to avoid tribal troubles etc. It was not at all clear that it would end by saying what the tribesmen most wanted to hear – namely that Seretse Khama was about to be restored to them.

When I got to Sefhare I could see that Gasebalwe Seretse had been absolutely correct. There had been trouble at this village in the early days of the 'Seretse troubles' and some villagers had beaten up a police detachment that had gone to arrest an 'agitator' – that is someone who thought Seretse should not have been exiled!

I was very nervous. There was a very large crowd and I thought the assembled villagers looked a pretty ugly bunch. There was a strong second hand smell of 'kaffir beer' floating up from the crowded kgotla. A hot wind was blowing and the air was full of swirling, gritty sand. I remember thinking that I would much rather be somewhere else.

Gasebalwe called the kgotla to order and told them to listen carefully because I had something important to tell them. I got to my feet and started reading from the wretched paper pausing after every sentence so that the interpreter could tell the silent villagers what it was all about. I had a pile of the printed announcements on the table in front of me and these started to blow about in the hot wind so I put my hand on top of the pile to secure them.

A particularly villainous looking individual sitting on the ground amongst those at the front caught my eye. He had a sparse and grizzled beard and despite the heat was wearing a tattered old khaki greatcoat. I noticed that he was trying to pull a rather large stone in front of him within reach with his knobkerrie. I feared the worst and looked at the poles behind me that formed the kgotla stockade and wondered how quickly I could get up and over them if the stones started to fly. I carried on watching the man with the knobkerrie out of the corner of my eye. Eventually when the stone was within reach he slowly leant forward and picked it up. I carried on reading the announcement but I was poised for flight to my truck. The old man got up slowly and came forward at a crouch with his free hand over his ear making that peculiar clicking sound with his tongue to signify his lower status, and put the stone on the pile of papers to prevent their blowing away. It is the only time in my life that I have felt the urge to kiss a man!

When we got to the end of the announcement and it dawned on the crowd that although Seretse had renounced the chieftain-ship he would be returning to Bechuanaland soon to live amongst them once more there was great jubilation. Gasebalwe Seretse stood up and facing the kgotla with his arms raised above his head shouted "Pula!" three times with great emphasis. The tribesmen responded and shouted "Pula" over and over again. This Setswana word means 'rain' but the Batswana use it to signify happiness, prosperity and all that makes life wonderful.

Gasebalwe Seretse escorted me to my truck in his usual courteous manner and taking off his hat bade me to "Tsamaya le Modimo" (Go with God) a supremely dignified Setswana farewell. I could sense that the old man was so pleased that at long last the tribe's dignity had been restored and I was proud that I had been the one to bring such good tidings to his people.

I made my way back to Mahalapye and having had a very long and a rather emotional day decided that a drink in the pub was called for. The usual crowd was gathered as though waiting for me. They had heard the rumours but they wanted the details. When I told them most of them thought that at last common sense had prevailed. One of them thought it was all wrong because the children would be coloured (that is of mixed race) and would never be accepted by the Bamangwato. I thought this was a bit rich because it was fairly common knowledge that the speaker was 'coloured' himself albeit from a long way back – I think he was born in St Helena – and everyone seemed to accept him. I held my tongue knowing it was fruitless to pursue a discussion when confronted with blind prejudice and anyway he didn't get much support from the rest of the bar crowd.

Seretse's return

Seretse Khama arrived back from exile on 10 October 1956. He flew in to Francistown from what was then Southern Rhodesia since he would not have been allowed to enter South Africa even if he had wanted to do so. He received a tremendous welcome and when he went to Serowe the next day he was again mobbed by an ecstatic crowd. When he reached the tribal offices as if to complete his homecoming, thunder and lightning rent the air and the rain came down in torrents.

About a week later I had just finished breakfast at my house in Mahalapye when a Chevrolet pick up truck coasted up my driveway and halted near the front door. I saw Rasebolai Kgamane climb out – he was the African Authority who carried out the functions of chieftainship. Seretse Khama followed him.

I had never met him and I was a bit apprehensive.

I knew Rasebolai Kgamane and I greeted him first. He introduced me to the soft-spoken Seretse and I invited them in. They said they had already breakfasted but accepted my offer of tea. We took this on the verandah and I noticed that a crowd was quickly gathering at my front gate. Rasebolai told me that they were going to address the Mahalapye kgotla and then go on to the other main villages in the Mahalapye area. They thought it proper that they should inform me in advance. I thought it was very courteous of them to inform me that they intended to hold meetings in their own tribal territory.

At that time my manservant was a Nyasa and when he brought the tray of tea out to the verandah he was of course totally respectful to my visitors but as far as he was concerned they were just visitors. But my housemaid was a Mongwato and when the news reached the kitchen that her chief was in the house she pattered out to the verandah in her bare feet and kneeling humbly and reverently before Seretse greeted him with deep emotion. He responded softly with exquisite courtesy and shook her proffered hand. It was immediately obvious to me why the Bamangwato adored him.

He didn't say much to me at our first meeting. He wasn't unfriendly but without any chatter I felt comfortable in his presence. Rasebolai asked whether I wanted to attend the Mahalapye meeting but I replied to the effect that I thought I would be rather surplus to their discussions and Seretse smiled his appreciation. When I escorted them to their truck I said goodbye to them in Setswana and Seretse smiled again. I remember thinking I could get to like this man very much.

Seretse's visit to Mahalapye and the surrounding villages was just the first of many visits he made to all parts of the tribal territory. On most of these his uncle Tshekedi and hordes of attendants and retainers accompanied him. The idea was to demonstrate to the tribesmen that the chieftainship dispute was over and life could now return to normal. A colleague of mine (Hugh Murray Hudson) accompanied the convoy on a trip it made to the far western villages – a trip, which lasted over a week because in those days the roads between villages were deep rutted tracks for the most part and negotiating them was slow and tedious.

Hugh told me that on the return journey at about six in the afternoon the convoy was ten or so miles from Serowe when Tshekedi who was in one of the leading trucks called a halt and said the convoy would camp there for the night. Seretse was towards the rear and he drove up to ask Tshekedi why they were pitching camp when they were so close to home. His uncle told him he had been in London too long and had obviously forgotten many tribal customs because no married Motswana would ever arrive home unannounced after sunset. Seretse told his uncle that it was just too bad if he didn't trust his wife because he (Seretse) most certainly did and he was carrying on which he did!

Not everyone welcomed Seretse and his wife Ruth back to Bechuanaland because there was still a lot of racial prejudice around. I heard odd rumours but as I was living a hundred miles or so away from Serowe I had little direct experience of it. I do know however that when the Serowe tennis club committee became aware that Ruth and Seretse intended to go to the annual dance it was cancelled on the grounds that it was too hot! I was also told that on one occasion when Ruth went into one of the trading stores to shop the wife of the trader asked her why she wasn't out at the lands (the arable areas) with the rest of her women. Ruth herself was harassed by the police for trivial matters concerning her car – a badly positioned rear light for instance.

Bruce Rutherford, the District Commissioner, was on overseas leave when Ruth and Seretse returned from exile and his place had been taken by Jimmy Allison who was a splendid fellow much liked by Seretse. Jimmy was one of the trio of District Officers who got into hot water in 1952 for writing a petition to the High Commissioner protesting at the British Government's treatment of Seretse and his family. When I was in Serowe I stayed with the Allisons who were just as generous and lavish in their hospitality as the Rutherfords.

On one of my visits Jimmy and I were transacting some business in his office when the OC Police barged in and said he intended to prosecute Ruth Khama under the liquor laws. Apparently she had bought a case of gin from the hotel in Palapye which was 40 miles away – in those days there was no hotel in Serowe – and she had not obtained a removal permit authorising her to do so.

What was bugging the OC of course was that no doubt Seretse would enjoy some of the gin and being a 'native' would be breaking the law. This emerged when Jimmy and I discussed the proposed prosecution with him. Jimmy tried hard to get the silly fellow to see sense but when he pompously starting sounding off about one law for the rich and one for the poor he was told to bugger off and find something useful to do.

I didn't get to know Seretse and Ruth very well at that time because shortly after their return to Bechuanaland I was told I was being transferred to Tshabong the desert station in the south west of Bechuanaland as I had been appointed District Commissioner of the Kgalagadi District. I was sorry to leave Mahalapye and the Tuli Block but at the same time was excited at the prospect of being in sole charge of this desert district. I was to get to know Seretse very well later in the 1960s.

GW on board the 'City of Paris' on his way out to Cape Town and the Bechuanaland Protectorate in 1954. Photograph by John Wilson.

A typical bush road in the Bechuanaland Protectorate. Photograph by Noel Redman.

*Top: the District Commissioner's Residency at Molepolole in
1948.*

*Below: the police post at Rakops in 1947. Photographs by Noel
Redman.*

Left: Tshekedi Khama in London in 1930 for discussions with the Colonial Secretary. Photographer unknown.

Below: a village school in the 1950s. This one is at Maunatlala. Photograph by Noel Redman.

From left: Chief Mokgosi of the Bamalete, Chief Bathoen of the Bangwaketsi and Regent Tshekedi Khama of the Bamangwato in 1947 at the time of the Royal visit.

Bruce Rutherford (standing left) and Agricultural Officer Wande surveying a dam site in 1947. Photographs by Noel Redman.

CHAPTER 4

THE KALAHARI

In 1956 Tshabong consisted of about a hundred huts, three or four wells, a trading store, two or three offices for government officials, a bungalow known as the Residency for the District Commissioner, another one for the police inspector and what were then referred to as 'staff lines' for the clerks and the police sergeant and constables.

This little settlement was on the edge of a flat depression about four miles across and six miles long which, when it rained – which was rarely – held water briefly in scattered pools. Further round the rim of this 'pan' as it was called, was the general trading store which belonged to a Mr Peacock, a splendid fellow, always ready to help and a good bush mechanic. This skill was particularly useful because the nearest garage was about 60 miles away in a village called Bray in South Africa. Bray also had the nearest liquor store.

About two hundred yards behind the staff lines there was a borehole which drew water from a depth of nearly 1000 feet to serve the needs of the government camp. The camel pens were near the borehole. A smart, youngish, Hottentot policeman looked after the herd of about forty camels. The camels were much used by the police on patrol. They were ill-tempered beasts but very useful – little escaped the keen eyes of the police when they rode through a village perched high up on their backs.

The government offices were in what used to be the District Commissioner's house. The police inspector and sergeant now occupied what had been the sitting room; the dining room and kitchen had been knocked together and formed my office. The former bedrooms and bathroom now housed the clerks and the various administrative records that were kept.

One Saturday afternoon in the mid-1930s when it was still the Residency, the District Commissioner and his wife were in the sitting room. He was holding a skein of wool and she was winding it into a ball. Outside a violent thunderstorm was raging. Suddenly there was a blinding flash of lightning, a fireball rolled down the chimney, engulfed the District Commissioner and killed him.

The distraught wife ran through the pouring rain to the police lines for help but, of course, there was nothing the police could do to help her husband. Although there was a truck on the station, the dead man had been the only one able to drive. In those days there was no radio link with headquarters. The police sergeant was at his wits end and the best he could do was to despatch a policeman by camel to get help from the nearest farm in South Africa – about thirty-five miles away.

Whenever there was a thunderstorm at Tshabong – which was not often – there were some spectacular effects. The lightning would bounce off the granite ridge that towered over the sand dunes behind the offices. When that happened, the police inspector always found something to talk to me about in my office and the sergeant found urgent business to transact with the clerks. During thunderstorms the former sitting room remained empty.

Station life

I had a very comfortable two-bedroomed bungalow with a small lawn in front and a splendid view of the flat, white pan. There was a gauzed verandah on the front and left hand side of the house which was a blessing in the hot weather. Its only disadvantage was that occasionally bats would get in through gaps in the eaves and fly about wildly. They were impossible to catch. Putting out the lights and opening the door didn't help as more bats would flock in, attracted perhaps by the fluttering within. My predecessor had been a squash Blue and used to swat the bats with an old squash racket. He had left this on the verandah and, to my lasting shame, I must admit that I too adopted this method of pest control.

I had other encounters with animals. Once in the middle of the night I felt hands moving over my face. I grabbed the arms, alarmed at the intrusion. However it was Sebogile, my house-servant who, finding me difficult to rouse, was groping for me in the dark to tell me there was "a cow in the bath". Half asleep I got up and made for the bathroom but Sebogile shouted to me from the back door to come outside.

Behind the house was a small swimming pool built by the squash Blue. It was bright moonlight outside and I was just in time to see a cow topple into the pool to join two of its companions. The poor beasts, crazed with thirst, had smashed through the fence. They could get their muzzles into the water only by leaning far over the small surrounding wall and this caused them to over balance. We roused the half dozen prisoners from the gaol and they hauled them out with much difficulty.

The prison was very small and could hold about ten men at a pinch. None of the prisoners was inside for anything very serious – stealing the odd goat or shooting big game were typical offences. The prison guard was called Sampson. He was a smart fellow and I think he had served in the army with the Batswana troops.

On Saturday mornings I had to inspect the prison and the

prisoners. Sampson would have them lined up waiting for me and to my embarrassment, would try to bring them up to attention when I approached. The prisoners, wearing their baggy shorts and long shirts, would snatch at their little prison hats and attempt to come to attention in an uncoordinated jumble of arms and legs.

I always asked if there were any complaints. On my first prison parade a prisoner said he was sick. He was constipated. I had been warned by the squash Blue that this was a common complaint. He had also told me that the medicines were kept in a tin box in the police office and the constipation cure was in a large bottle.

I went and got the bottle from the police office which was empty at the time because the sergeant was inspecting the police lines. I gave the prisoner a generous spoonful. When I was returning the bottle to the box the police sergeant came in and very politely asked what I was doing. I told him and he informed me that the medicine I had used was for the camels.

I watched the prisoner carefully for a few days but to my immense relief he seemed to suffer no ill-effects. He must have enjoyed the results because he, along with two others, reported sick the next Saturday. This time the correct dose was given.

Tshabong was a lonely station – especially for a bachelor – but it had a beauty which is easy to describe yet hard to understand. Most of the time it was hot and bone dry. The pan and the settlement were half rimmed by golden sand dunes. The vegetation was sparse. The night skies were spectacular and the silence in the evenings and early mornings was absolute. It was very remote.

During my first days there I felt very, very lonely. The police inspector was on long leave and I was the only European on the station and indeed in the whole village. I was 26 years old and I enjoyed company but in those days racial segregation was complete.

Apart from candles, paraffin lamps were the only form of lighting I had. When my newly purchased Aladdin lamp became hot, the wick vibrated and it made a low moaning sound. I figured this out later but before I did so I thought the noise was the sound of an approaching truck. Out would come the drinks and the ice (from the paraffin refrigerator) for the visitor who never appeared!

But I learnt to read the night. I knew the sounds – springbok coughing on the pan and the bats and plovers. There was a very steep sand dune about five miles down the track which led to my bungalow and in order to get up and over it it was necessary to put your truck in low gear and your foot down hard on the accelerator. I was soon able to recognise the noise of a gear change and a whining engine as a vehicle negotiated this dune. After a few months when the loneliness had entered my soul, if I heard these sounds, I would put out the lights and go to bed if I wasn't expecting a visitor, hoping that I wouldn't be disturbed.

Tiny as it was, Tshabong was the headquarters of a vast administrative district nearly 60,000 square miles in extent but with a population of only about 20,000. In other words it was an area about the size of England and Wales with the population of a small market town.

Outsiders used to like to visit Tshabong to get a taste of the desert. Some were government officials and their visits were generally useful because I could often persuade them into acts of generosity – for instance some fencing poles from the Director of Veterinary Services to enclose a village well to prevent damage by cattle.

Some of my visitors were less welcome. I remember one earnest German academic who was an anthropologist from the University of Pretoria. He was convinced that there was a lost city in the Kalahari and was determined to find traces of ancient civilisations in the desert. He became very excited when he discovered a regular pattern of stone circles dotted around the pan in front of my house and spent about a week mapping them. He gave me a rough copy of the sketch map before he departed and left me in peace – much to my relief because he had a voracious appetite.

When I next visited the headquarters about two hundred miles away, I showed this sketch to 'Lawrie' Lawrenson – the senior official I had stayed with when I first arrived in Mafikeng. He was very interested in Tshabong because his father-in-law, who had been in the police, had established the first police post there in the late 1920s. He had himself been stationed there in the early 1930s as a police inspector. When he got married he had to get special permission for his bride to join him because his thatched wattle and daub living quarters were not considered by those in authority in those days to be suitable for a white woman.

He studied the sketch very carefully and asked me a few questions about where this and that circle was in relation to other landmarks shown on the map – Peacock's store or van der Westhuizen's well for instance. He then told me that the 'prehistoric stone circles' were golf tees which he had got the prisoners to scrape out for him so that he could practice his golf when he was stationed there. I never heard from the anthropologist again – somebody in Pretoria must have disillusioned him.

I held meetings with the villagers in Tshabong whenever there was something important to discuss. These were held in the meeting place that was an open-ended semi-circular stockade known as the kgotla. A chair and a table were always provided for me and chairs for any visiting government officials.

Mr Peacock usually attended these meetings and when he did I enjoyed watching him walking to the gathering from his store followed by his rather surly teenage son carrying a chair for his father. The ordinary villagers sat on the ground, the headmen had low stools and Mr Peacock had a chair. When the meeting was assembled a messenger would be sent for me.

When the need arose I held similar meetings in the various villages scattered throughout the district. The desert people often needed help and had to be visited regularly to find out what their needs were. Life was hard and most of them were very poor. It was often possible to improve the quality of their life considerably by the simplest of measures. They were proud and independent. When the need arose they willingly provided free labour to build a classroom or a small dispensary or some other communal building with the cement, timber and other materials that I was able to provide out of my small budget.

Travelling around this huge district took much time because the 'roads' were simply rough tracks ground into the desert by trucks and settlements were far apart. For instance the 170 miles journey from Tshabong to Tshane – the sub-headquarters in the north – took about fourteen hours and most of the time the truck was grinding through heavy sand in low gear.

This travelling would have been tedious despite the marvellous landscape and the vast herds of springbok, gemsbok, eland and hartebeest which roamed over the desert savannah but for the fact that I always had a wonderful companion in the person of my friend Bok.

My friend Bok

I first met Bok a few days after I arrived in Tshabong. He came to my office looking for a job presumably having heard there was a vacancy for a messenger-interpreter. He was about ten years older than I was, tall, slim and very erect. His skin was brown over deep yellow and he spoke good English in slow, deep and measured tones. He had a diagonal scar gouged across his nose and down his left cheek. I took to him at once.

He told me he spoke several languages – Hottentot, Afrikaans, Setswana and some Bushman. He seemed ideal – in fact he was so good that I wondered why he was applying for the job which wasn't very well paid. I told him to come back the next day and I would tell him what I had decided.

When I spoke to the sergeant who, in the absence of the inspector, was in charge of the police station, he told me that Bok was an ex-police corporal who had been dismissed from the force because of a criminal conviction. He advised me against hiring him. I asked what crime he had committed and was told that whilst on patrol in a European farming area in the east of the country he had poached a kudu – a large antelope.

I went back to my office and thought about this and decided that for a man brought up in the desert to shoot a kudu was the equivalent of an English schoolboy going scrumping in an orchard. I decided to hire Bok but not to say too much about him to the personnel people in the faraway headquarters in Mafikeng.

When the clerk brought him into my office the next morning he stood in front of my desk and, without exactly saluting, seemed to come to full attention. I told him he had the job. He displayed no emotion. I asked him why he had not told me about the kudu. He said I had not asked him about his previous employment and in any case he knew that I would find out about it before I came to a decision. That put me in my place and he withdrew.

When I looked out of the office window a little while later he had driven the Ford truck within reach of the standpipe behind the office, taken off the khaki jacket of the messenger's uniform that had been issued to him and was washing and polishing the truck. I knew I had made the right choice.

From then on Bok accompanied me on all my trips. We usually spent two or three weeks in every month travelling around the district because this was the only way of keeping in touch with the people. It always intrigued me that whilst I would set off with several trunks containing clothes, bedding, food and cooking equipment and camp chairs, tables, bed, and canvas bath and wash basin, all he would take was a blanket roll containing some spare clothes in addition to his blankets, with his soap in a tin box, a razor and toothbrush and a knife, fork, spoon, mug and plate. He also took two small, three-legged, iron cooking pots. He always looked smart, even after the longest trip.

He didn't talk much when we were driving along but he was a comfortable companion. When he did speak I listened because he was telling me something I needed to know – there was a lion under that tree or there was a springbok ram near the road ahead and we needed meat. Sometimes it would be some interesting bit of district gossip – for instance why an unmarried school mistress had resigned and the name of the prospective father.

He rarely laughed but always chuckled with sheer delight whenever we drove past a meerkat colony. He obviously found it terribly funny the way these little animals scurried about in confusion and stood up straight-backed on their hind legs to get a better view of the danger.

On tour in the desert

Having been born in the desert Bok knew never to take liberties with it and I followed his example. Whenever I left on tour I always made sure the police knew where we were going and when we expected to return and I used the police radio to contact the police posts at Tshane in the north and Werda in the east. There was a Public Works Department driver who neglected to take these precautions. His truck broke down and he started to walk the 50 or so miles to Tshabong. He was in a very bad way when an Afrikaans farmer from the other side of the Molopo came across him. This farmer was probably poaching – the farmers could listen in on their wirelesses to the police radio so they had a rough idea when the coast was clear and no trucks were out on patrol – but he saved the driver's life. The lorry labourer who had stayed with the truck was in quite good shape when he was picked up.

One of the first lessons Bok taught me was that in order to get around in the desert tyre pressures had to be low – not more that 19 lbs per square inch. We once came across a couple of young lads from some voluntary organisation who were on a familiari-sation tour and had crossed into our district from the north. They were frantic because they were making such slow progress and the radiator of their truck kept boiling. After they had explained what a desperate time they had had even when they were not in heavy sand, Bok got out the pressure gauge and tested their tyres and found them to be in the high 30s. He deflated them to 20 and the lads tested their truck. They were amazed at the progress they made.

They also told me that they had camped one night and because it was a beautiful evening they didn't bother with a tent and pitched their sleeping bags next to the fire. One of them woke up in the middle of the night and as he was lying wondering what had disturbed him he heard a snuffling noise. Arching his head up from his recumbent position he saw a huge lion sniffing at the bottom of his companion's sleeping bag. He flopped back and in a hoarse whisper told his companion "Joe, there is a lion sniffing at your feet". The quavering reply was "I know!" But the lion moved on and they scuttled into their Landrover. They decided against sleeping in the open in the future.

Bok told me that once one of my predecessors came across an African family that had run into big trouble on the Tshabong to Tshane track. The father was making for Tshane with his wife and his two pre-teenage children. They were travelling by mule cart. The father knew the road well and was reckoning on filling up with water at the Mabuasehuba well about 70 miles north of Tshabong. When he arrived at the well he found the water undrinkable because a hyena had tumbled in and drowned and its putrid body was floating in it.

He pressed on because he knew that there were usually lots of tsamma melons to the north of the well and juice could be extracted from them. It is odd that he expected his mule to survive on them but I suppose he had no choice because there were no wells for 70 miles north and south of him. When he got to the tsamma area he could see by the spoor that a large herd of springok and many gemsbok had beaten him to it and withered melon skins were all that remained of his emergency water supply.

However, he was a resourceful man and he buried his wife and children up to their necks in the sand in the shade of a large thorn tree to prevent then from becoming too dehydrated. This is what my predecessor came upon as he was making his way north to Tshane. The mule was alive – just – and the family was in a desperately bad way. They all survived.

Tshane

Tshane was a small settlement consisting of a police station with the formidable Sergeant Major Bokowe in charge and a few dozen scattered huts near a couple of wells. There was also a three-teacher school. The police post was on the edge of a huge pan the colour of bleached bones and dead flat – so flat and large that aeroplanes could land there easily.

One did so once. A South African Airways Dakota, en route from Windhoek to Johannesburg, developed engine trouble and landed there – much to the astonishment of the locals who had heard aeroplanes but had never seen one on the ground before.

When I read the radio message from Sergeant Major Bokowe informing me of the exciting event, I thought at first he had been on this lonely station for too long. But when I spoke to him on the two-way radio he seemed normal and told me the bird had flown.

I used to visit Tshane about once a month. I never tired of sitting outside the guest rondavel in the evenings watching the emptiness of the huge pan that stretched out before me. There was a store near the camp owned by an Indian. It was remarkably well stocked seeing that it was in such an isolated place. I think it depended heavily on returning mine labourers who when they arrived back at the end of their contracts had pockets full of deferred pay. When the storekeeper discovered that I liked curry he made sure that I was very well fed on several occasions during my visits and the meals he sent over to my rondavel in the evenings in neat aluminium stacking pans were simply delicious. I am afraid I couldn't say the same about the tea he would insist on my having when I called in at the store during trading hours. It was always served with hot milk and spices – cumin I think – and took ages to cool. I occasionally made small purchases from his store and as I rarely carried cash he would bill me for these monthly. My bill would be waiting when I arrived and was always addressed to Sir George Winstanley – I rather liked that!

On one of my visits I discovered some old Occurrence Books in the police storeroom. These were in effect station diaries and contained a day by day account of station life as seen by the post commander. Most of the entries were very mundane but now and again gems appeared. I remember one entry from the early 1930s. The post commander then was a young white trooper called Emmanuel Clark. He must have lead a desperately lonely life stuck away in Tshane with no motorised transport and no radio contact. In one entry he recorded that Corporal Preston Whyte and Trooper McDermott had arrived that afternoon on camels from Tshabong with the mail and "a case of brandy". There was no entry in the Occurrence Book for several days. I was particularly interested in this record because when I knew them the trooper and his visitors were grizzled veteran superintendents – all of them prodigious drinkers.

I sometimes had the company of the stock inspector who was stationed at Werda in the south east of the district near the dry bed of the Molopo river. He was a huge Afrikaner called Ferreira. He was over six feet six inches and must have weighed 16 stones or more. Naturally he was known as Tiny. He professed to be intensely loyal to the British and I think he probably was. Rumour had it that he made an emergency delivery of his son on the verandah of his house at Werda and when he caught the boy he cradled him in his huge hands, turned him towards the distant Mafikeng and told him to salute the flag. I didn't believe this when I first heard it but Mrs Tiny told me it was true.

Tiny's strength was prodigious and I once saw him hoist a 44 gallon drum of petrol on to the back of his truck unaided. He was usually very slow at starting in the morning. On one occasion when we were preparing to go on a trip together I went over to his truck to remonstrate with him about his tardiness and saw him booting one of his assistants up the backside to try and hurry things along. I decided that I would speak to him about this later. That night after supper whilst we were sitting round the campfire chatting, Tiny, clasping his huge hands together reverentially, told me that before he went to sleep each night he always said a prayer for "the little brown people". I didn't tell him I didn't believe him because I realised he was apologising for what I had witnessed earlier in the day.

He was a superb bush cook and his pot roast venison joint was a wonder to taste. He needed a lot of food to sustain him. Soon after I arrived in Tshabong the police inspector told me he thought Tiny was overshooting on his pot licence – because we were on such a remote station we were allowed to shoot one head of big or two head of small game per week for the pot. I said I would size up the situation and speak to him if necessary. After I had been out on tour twice with Tiny and saw how much he ate I told the inspector I would rather have an energetic stock inspector than one faint with hunger and I heard no more about how he took advantage of his pot licence.

Tiny enjoyed a drink in the evenings round the campfire – he once told me that what the Kalahari took out of you during the day it put it all back in the evening – but I never saw him the worse for wear. However, I believe he went downhill later. His director, hearing rumours about his drinking, decided to investigate and went with him on one of his trips down the Molopo. He told me he noticed that Tiny frequently drank from the canvas water bottle hanging from the side mirror – which he could reach without stopping the truck – but thought nothing of it as it was a ferociously hot day. When they arrived at their destination the director, needing to quench his thirst, took a long swig from the water bag only to find he was drinking strong watered-down brandy. Tiny was moved to a less lonely station and learnt to behave himself. He might have been up to the same tricks when I travelled with him but I will never know because I never sampled his water bag.

A very curious thing happened on one of my visits to Tshane. There was a small camel herd there and one was very sick. Tiny, who was very good with livestock, decided it would have to be destroyed. He took it off into the bush some way from the camp and did what he had to do. He told the camel herd to keep the remainder of the herd away from the place of slaughter but his instructions were either misunderstood or ignored. One of the camels stumbled upon the mess and took off like the wind.

I was told later that after a day or two it had not returned so the police organised a search party and two of them set off on camels and followed the spoor. They were amazed to find that it was heading straight for Bokspits and in fact recaptured it about 10 miles from this settlement. The camel had been born at Witdraai, the South African Police camel breeding station, about two miles from Bokspits. The Bechuanaland Police bought its embryonic camel herd from Witdraai and moved it about 100 miles east to Tshabong and a few months later moved a section of the herd 170 miles north to Tshane. The runaway camel was part of this herd. When it was severely frightened many years later it made straight for home – not the way it had come but along the hypotenuse of the triangle.

A visit to Mrs Bok

Tshane was Bok's home village. The day after we arrived on my first visit, he came to me in the late afternoon and said his mother wished to come and see me. I said that I would love to meet her.

He said the trouble was she walked with great difficulty because she had arthritic knees. I said in that case I would have to visit her. Bok sprang into action. I heard him shouting at the man who swept the sandy surrounds of the police offices and saw the fellow go scampering off through the bushes. He had obviously been sent to warn Mrs Bok.

We set off and soon came to the huts that formed Bok's kraal. Bok approached carefully calling out softly to warn those inside that we were approaching. He drew me through an open gate in the fence that surrounded the courtyard that in turn surrounded the largest hut. The yard was beautifully swept and Mrs Bok was sitting on a skin mat in the shade of the hut. Her skin was mahogany coloured and she was deeply wrinkled. She was wearing colourful clothes – a loose top and a long voluminous skirt. Wrapped around her head was a brightly coloured cloth that was not unlike a turban. If I had met her in Spain I would have put her down as a gypsy.

She greeted me in a most dignified manner and spoke briefly to a young girl who was obviously waiting on her. This girl got up immediately, brought me a low, folding, locally-made stool and then disappeared behind the hut. She returned almost at once carrying a tray on which was a cup of tea, a bowl of sugar and a small jug of milk – all covered with a net cloth decorated around the edges with coloured beads. The tea was for me.

After I had helped myself to milk and sugar the old woman started to speak with Bok acting as the interpreter. She said how sad she had been when her youngest son had been dismissed from his important government post, that he was a good boy despite the trouble he had caused and how grateful she was to me for giving him another chance. It was odd to listen to Bok interpreting this as though he were speaking about some other person. I can't remember what I said in reply but it obviously pleased her because she inclined her head courteously.

After I had drunk the tea and we had finished talking I said it was time for me to be getting back. Turning her head a little so that she was looking over my shoulder, she said something in a slightly raised voice and the young girl produced a paper parcel that she gave to her. Mrs Bok gave it me and said it was a small present as a mark of her gratitude. It was a beautiful mat made out of a black and white calf skin with an exquisitely decorated soft springbok leather surround. The old woman had stitched and embroidered it herself.

When we came out of the courtyard, a well-built man of about fifty who had been squatting in the shade of a large thorn tree got up and taking off his hat came towards us. He had a withered right arm but otherwise looked fit and very strong. Bok introduced him and he held out his left arm for the handshake. It was his brother, Harry Bok.

On tour in the Kalahari

When Bok and I were on tour and between villages, we stopped to make camp at about five o'clock in the evening. He always chose the campsite which had to have not only plenty of dead wood nearby but wood of a type which burned hot and left good ashes. When he had decided he would tap on the dashboard and I would pull off the track.

In no time he had a tarpaulin down, a chair out and a table with checked tablecloth set up. On the table would be a glass and a bottle of Cape brandy. A canvas water bag would have been transferred from the arm of a side mirror of the truck to a low branch nearby. He would then set about collecting the wood and making the fire. I once seized an axe and started to help with the wood – Bok simply took it from me and told me to go and have a drink. I never interfered again.

Night comes early and swiftly in the Kalahari but long before darkness fell the fire would be burning brightly, the paraffin lamps lit and the supper - usually a stew - cooking. After we had eaten we would settle round the fire, light our pipes, and then Bok would become talkative. He was very inquisitive and used to ask questions about England – was it true that in London the trains ran under the ground, where did the Queen live, was she rich, where did I live when I was a boy?

Once when I described some part of my boyhood, I mentioned the limestone caves near Castelton in Derbyshire – I said the main one used to be called Ye Devil's Arse. Bok and Sebogile – who was an eager listener – laughed until the tears streamed down their cheeks.

Often when we were camped out in the desert far away from any settlements, Bok, who had very acute hearing, would murmur to me without turning his head, "They are coming Morena" – "they" being the Bushmen.

They would have heard our truck from far off and would have known when we stopped. Then they would have started walking because they knew we would have water and probably tobacco. They would hover just outside the circle of light from our fire as they sized up the situation and, having decided we were safe, would flit forwards like little brown shadows. Bok once told me that they always left their weapons - bows and arrows, spears and knobkerries - under a bush in the shadows outside the range of the light from our fire because it would have been bad manners to bring them into our camp.

They always brought containers for water – ostrich egg shells, bottles, cans, or gourds. Bok would help them fill up whatever they had. We always had a bag of leaf tobacco and he would give them a couple of handfuls and some sugar in a screw of paper – how their almond-shaped eyes in their delicate, high cheek-boned, oval faces glittered when these delicacies were produced.

They always sat in a group with one slightly in front of the others; he would receive whatever was offered and pass it back. Nobody ever asked for anything. They never stayed for long and, after a short while, they would slip back into the night – I suppose they would have a long walk back to the rest of the band who, no doubt, would be eagerly awaiting their return.

I never saw Bok drink strong liquor – it was against the law then for Africans to drink "European" liquor but I don't know what he was. Only a small part of him could have been African and as a 'Coloured' (that is, a person of mixed race) it was legal for him to drink. He never did drink in my presence although Sebogile – who usually came with us on our trips – once confided in me that Bok had quite a thirst when he was off duty!

He was right because I once saw Bok suffering from a monumental hangover. We were in Tshane and I had told him I wanted to leave before sunrise because it was a long, hard drive to Tshabong. He was late the next morning and I was standing by the truck when he arrived. I gave him a roasting and he looked very sheepish. The sun was rising when we left and Bok said he would sit in the back of the truck. I noticed that he soon fell asleep.

About half an hour out of Tshane I saw a springbok about seventy yards ahead. We needed meat and I stopped the truck and got the rifle from behind the seat. It was a standard, police-issue .303. I suddenly thought I would put one over on Bok. Sober, he was a splendid shot and I thought I would teach him a lesson. I woke him up and told him I would give him ten shillings if he could shoot the buck through the head from a standing shot. Ten shillings was quite a lot of money in those days.

Bok climbed down rather shakily, looking more yellow than he normally did, took the rifle and, with legs apart, settled his feet in the sand. He took careful aim and fired. The springbok dropped like a stone. I lost my ten shillings and Bok slept most of the way to Tshabong.

But most of the time Bok was at his helpful best and he never missed a trick. Once I had to recuse myself from hearing a court case because I had prior knowledge of what had led to a serious assault at Lehututu – a village near Tshane. A effete District Officer was sent to hear the case. We were a bit late setting out from Tshabong for Tshane and I said we would camp at Mabuasehuba pan, about half way. When we were about to set off the young DO asked whether we were taking a tent and I replied rather scornfully saying we did not need one because it didn't rain in the Kalahari in May. When we were setting up camp that evening Bok sidled up to me and in a low voice said "It is going to rain Morena". And it certainly did rain around midnight. Bok and I dragged our blankets under the truck and the delicate one spent an uncomfortable upright night in the front of the truck. Bok didn't laugh in front of him the next morning but I could tell he was very amused.

School visits

I always took a special interest in the schools in the district. In those days most of them were very modest indeed and it was not unusual, in the smaller settlements, for one teacher to try and teach several classes. It was difficult to get good teachers for these primitive schools and we often had to make do with very mediocre people many of who had fallen foul of the education authorities in South Africa for drunkenness, incompetence or whatever. But our salaries were so low and most of our schools so remote that we had virtually to take whatever was on offer.

I remember one teacher in particular who taught in a one-teacher school in a village on a desolate stony ridge overlooking the dry riverbed of the Molopo. That we had been able to find a teacher to live there was a source of wonder to me. Once, after we had spent the night in camp near this village, I decided to pay a surprise visit to the school. We arrived at the school at about ten o'clock but it was deserted. After I had checked with Bok that it was Friday and not a public holiday, we went in search of the teacher.

Eventually we tracked him down. He was quite obviously drunk and he greeted me in a slurred voice. Bok spoke to him sharply and he snatched off his hat so I suppose he had been given an instruction. This seemed to sober him up a little. I asked why the school was closed and he said the goats had eaten the Friday part of the timetable that he had pinned to the outside of the door to the one classroom school.

He stood there, grinning uneasily, waiting for his fate to be pronounced. I was so impressed by the ingenuity of the excuse that he had hatched in his drink-befuddled brain that, instead of dismissing him, I told him to pull himself together and make sure the school opened promptly on Monday and stayed open.

We then returned to the truck. Bok said nothing but I could tell by the way he was walking – rather stiffly and a little in front of me – that he thought I had done rather badly.

But on other occasions my actions met with his approval. On one of our visits to Bokspits – a village in the south-west hand corner of Bechuanaland inhabited by Coloured people and set amongst towering sand dunes – we paid a courtesy call on the school. It was a very good little school considering how remote the village was from other parts of the country. The community was very progressive and quite wealthy because they farmed karakul sheep. They were great at self-help and had built the school themselves. The headmaster was good at his job but a bit of a weasel. He had come to us from somewhere in the Cape Province and I think he had got into trouble by financing his love of the bottle by dipping into the school sports fund.

When the children had assembled to greet us I noticed that there was one little girl who had fair hair and very blue eyes. I remarked on this to Steenkamp – the headmaster – and he said her name was Martin. He added that she got her colouring from her "grandfather" and spitefully added that he was not supposed to be in the country but, with a jerk of his head, said he was "over there" with his granddaughter.

We finished our school business and as we were leaving the school I asked Bok what this "grandfather" business was all about. He told me that the old man was in fact the child's great grandfather and he had landed up in the Bokspits area after the Boer War. He was a bit of a scallywag and eked out a living selling liquor to the locals and poaching and selling the skins wherever he could. Eventually a zealous police inspector at Tshabong had him declared a prohibited immigrant in Bechuanaland. I said we should pay him a visit.

When we reached the little group of buildings that formed the homestead pointed out by Steenkamp with his long chin, there was a youngish women standing by the gate. I guessed she was the mother of the little blue eyed girl. I asked where the old man was and with a bowed head she took me into the yard. In a corner sitting on an upright chair was an old man who was quite well dressed in a seafaring manner and smoking a pipe. We exchanged a few pleasantries and his accent was as strong as the day he sailed away to the Boer War from Plymouth. Then I said I understood he was not supposed to be in Bechuanaland and he explained that he was getting on a bit (he must have been in his 80s) and his grandson's family was looking after him because he couldn't manage on his own. After a bit more chit-chat I said I had better be going and bade him farewell. As I turned to go he said in his broad west country accent "You're not going to send me back are you son?" I told him that I had a poor memory and sometimes couldn't remember the people I had met. This little transaction met with Bok's approval.

In Court at Tshabong

When I presided in court Bok had to interpret when languages other than English were used. He was then always stiff and formal. I suppose, with his history, he knew only too well that the courtroom was a place for serious business.

He was a very good interpreter but sometimes translation of certain terms had him foxed. In the Tswana language there are words for a few simple, basic colours but when it comes to describing the different colours of cattle (and sheep and goats), bewildering combinations of colours can be described by one or two words.

Once, in a stock theft case, I noticed that Bok was wrestling with a description. He finally informed me that the bull was black with black spots. In fact it was black with white patches which were mottled with black streaks and blotches but in Setswana there was one word to describe this.

On one occasion in court I actually saw something approaching a smile quiver around his lips. An old man was charged with hunting royal game. He was so old and decrepit that I doubted whether he could have hunted a flea let alone a huge buck but he had been found in possession of an eland skin.

The old man was called August January and despite the fact that he was of mixed race, he was very, very black. He was wearing a pair of big blue sunglasses with a label reading "Made in Hong Kong" stuck diagonally across one of the lenses – no doubt these had been bought in Peacock's store. I began reading out the charge and Bok was interpreting into Setswana but after a couple of sentences I noticed that the old man was very agitated.

I asked what was bothering him and he said in a dialect of Afrikaans, "Eksuus sier. Ek praat nie die kaffir taal nie". It was when Bok translated this that he almost smiled because it meant "Excuse me sir. I don't speak the kaffir language". I can't remember what sentence I imposed but I am sure the old man was neither fined nor imprisoned.

Another court adventure concerned two Afrikaans farmers from across the border who had been caught by the police shooting springbok in Bechuanaland. Poaching by people from across the southern border was rife – the border was easy to cross because it was unfenced and simply indicated by heaps of whitewashed stones running down the bed of the Molopo river which flowed very rarely.

An attorney from Vryburg defended the two farmers and there was some dispute about exactly where the alleged offence had occurred. Determined that justice must not only be done but must be seen to be done, I decided to adjourn to the place of the alleged crime, which was about 60 miles from Tshabong, so that we could re-enact the scene on the ground. This we did.

The farmers stood where they had been standing and a sack was placed where the springbok had been grazing when it was shot through the heart. The police sergeant agreed that these placings were correct. The wily attorney then demonstrated, by reference to the beacons, that the shooting had taken place in South Africa – just inside certainly, but not in Bechuanaland. I acquitted the accused and they departed in the attorney's pick-up truck leaving behind them a cloud of dust.

Some months later I was in the bar of the hotel in Bray when I got into conversation with a local farmer who had taken a drop too much. He told me with great enjoyment that the day before the springbok case, the two accused had carefully shifted the stones marking the border. When I told Bok later how we had been outwitted, he made no comment but I could tell he was very impressed.

Kalahari ghosts

The last trip I made with Bok was particularly memorable. I was due to go on overseas leave and knew that on my return I would be posted to the far northwest – the land of water and the Okavango wetlands.

I had to go to Bokspits in the southwest corner of Bechuanaland to settle some grazing dispute among the villagers. After my business there I wanted to go north through the Gemsbok National Park which straddled the South Africa/Bechuanaland border, following the dry bed of the Nossob until I reached Union's End where Bechuanaland, South Africa and South West Africa met.

I wanted to visit this place because, at the beginning of the twentieth century, a large German camel patrol had been wiped out there by the Hottentots. The patrol had made its last stand at the water hole called Groot Kalk. It was said to be haunted by the ghosts of German sentries calling out their challenge, "Wer ist dort?". I had a rough sketch map of the area that had been given to me by a policeman who had visited the spot but had not camped there. This intrigued me.

Bok was quite keen – rather to my surprise. I guess there was quite a lot of Hottentot in him. He could certainly speak the language very well. He came up trumps with his discovery that the grandfather of the Hottentot who looked after the camel herd at Tshabong had actually been with the band when it had surrounded the Germans at Groot Kalk. This wizened little man was around seventy so he must have been a lad of ten or so at the time. He agreed to come with us as a guide.

After settling our business at Bokspits and spending the night there, we set off north. It was late May so it was cooling down and although the chances of rain were never very high in the Kalahari, they were much less in the winter. We had been driving along for half an hour or so when Bok told me to look under a large baobab tree just off the track in front of us. There was a pride of lions including a magnificent black-maned male. They had obviously killed and eaten during the night and were enjoying the early morning sun. We carried on. The dry valley was teeming with game – gemsbok, springbok and hartebeest. After another half hour or so, we came upon another pride of lions.

When we stopped for a break around noon, I heard the old Hottentot talking to Bok who actually laughed at what he said. Later, as he was siphoning petrol into the truck from the drum on the back, he told me that the old man had said that the lions would have eaten him (he was sitting on the back of the open truck) but they didn't because they were afraid of the District Commissioner!

Late in the afternoon when we were well up the Nossob we came to a widening of the valley. The Hottentot drummed on the roof of the truck and we stopped. Bok, leaning out of the window, exchanged a few words with him then turned to me and said the old man had said that this was the place. From my sketch map I knew that Groot Kalk was about five miles further on so Bok said something to the old man and we continued.

We came to Union's End at about five in the afternoon. As we drew close, clouds were building up. Bok didn't say anything but I could sense that he was uneasy. He was staring straight ahead with his battered trilby hat pulled down low over his eyes. We came to a slight rise and on reaching the crest there was our destination – Groot Kalk – nestling in a large saucer-shaped depression.

We slowed down and from the truck were starting to look around for a campsite when we heard a long, low, menacing rumble of thunder. Lightning flickered on the horizon. Below us a spotted hyena broke cover and see-sawed across the depression with its loping run, making its wandering cry of "Who-oof" which starts low and ends on a high, loud note.

The old Hottentot was terrified. He had covered his head with a blanket. I told Bok to get him in the cab with us. Sebogile wasn't very happy on the back of the truck either but that was because he thought it was going to rain. However the clouds rolled away and after giving the Hottentot a cigarette and re-assuring him that no ghosts would dare come near the District Commissioner, we made camp but I noticed that he and Bok made two large fires.

Later that evening we persuaded the old man to tell us what had happened so long ago at Groot Kalk. I had read about the incident before but it was fascinating to hear it confirmed by an eyewitness.

A large German camel patrol of about 40 men had set out on a punitive expedition to deal with a band of Hottentots under their headman Simon Kooper. This band had been maiming and rustling cattle in revenge for the many cruelties inflicted on the Hottentots by the Germans who then ruled South West Africa.

The Hottentots, who were splendid bush men, kept just in front of the Germans. They led them on and when they established camp at the big water hole – Groot Kalk – they surrounded them. The saucer shape of the depression was ideal for this manoeuvre. The Germans could not make a break for it because the Hottentots pinned them down with withering rifle fire.

After a siege that lasted about two weeks, the Germans were desperate because both their rations and ammunition were running low. They proposed a truce and the Hottentots agreed that if they laid down their arms they could return to Windhoek.

The Germans came out of their camp without their arms but the Hottentots took their camels and their clothes and told them to walk back naked to Windhoek – about 200 miles away. They set off but none reached the top of the ridge – the Hottentots shot them all down. A savage tale, but the Germans had treated the Hottentots ferociously in the past.

A tale of a leopard

As we were sitting thinking about what we had just heard, I looked at Bok and the flickering shadows of the firelight threw the scar on his nose and cheek into sharp relief. I asked if he would mind telling me how he got these scars as I had often wondered what had caused them and would be going away shortly. I did not want to do so with my curiosity unsatisfied.

He told me that he and his brother Harry had cattle at Tshane and many years ago they started losing calves. One morning Harry came to him and said that another calf had been taken and he had seen the tracks of a large leopard leading away from the cattle kraal. He and Bok set out to track and kill the leopard. Harry had his shotgun and Bok collected his donkey.

They followed the tracks of the leopard until they disappeared into a large, dense, circular, thorn thicket. Bok rode right round and saw no tracks leading out of it. When he got back to Harry he told him to stay where he was with the shotgun while he rode around the thicket again shouting this time to make the leopard break cover.

When Bok was on the opposite side of the thicket to Harry he heard screams and a savage snarling. He trotted as fast as he could on his donkey – donkeys can't gallop – and when he rounded the thicket was appalled to see the leopard on top of his brother with its teeth sunk into his upper arm.

Bok couldn't see the gun and as he was sure that the leopard was getting the better of Harry, he jumped off the donkey and seized the leopard by the tail in an effort to haul it off. The leopard spun around, clawed him across the face, knocked him to the ground and sank its teeth into his shoulder.

Harry, who had been lying on the gun, jumped up, grabbed it with his good arm and somehow managed to shove the barrel in the beast's ear and blew its head off. That was how Bok got his scarred face and Harry his withered arm.

In conclusion, Bok advised me that if ever I had to catch a leopard by its tail, I must never pull but push because that would make it go forward – the same as a cat he said. I looked at him closely as he lit his pipe with a hot coal from the fire. He was absolutely serious.

I need hardly add that we heard no ghostly German sentries that night. I suppose the old Hottentot thought that the District Commissioner had kept them away!

Above: aerial view of the government settlement at Tshabong in 1954. The Residency is in the centre front of the picture.

Below: Tshane Pan. Both photographs by MRB Williams.

Left: the road from Tshabong to Tshane.

Below: Headmen of the Kgalagadi District at Tshabong in 1955. Photograph by MRB Williams.

Above: GW on a police camel with unknown policeman at Lehututu in 1956. Photograph by MRB Williams.

Left: the kgotla at Lehututu in 1956. Photograph by G. Winstanley.

Above: a Bushman camp in the Kalahari

Above: on tour in the Kalahari.
Both photographs by G. Winstanley

CHAPTER 5

POSTED TO NGAMILAND

I returned from my first overseas leave towards the end of 1957. The last few weeks of my five months spell had dragged because I was beginning find the idleness tiresome. I was also anxious to get back because I had been told my next posting was Ngamiland. This district was in the far northwest of Bechuanaland bounded by South West Africa in the west and the Caprivi Strip in the north. Across the Strip was Angola, then administered after a fashion by Portugal. I was eagerly looking forward to my new posting. I had heard many tales about the peculiarities of many of the residents there and was looking forward to meeting them. Another reason why I was anxious to get to my new posting was that Ngamiland had in abundance what was lacking over the rest of the country – namely water.

However, I had to curb my impatience because when I disembarked at Cape Town there was a message waiting for me instructing me to report to headquarters in Mafikeng instead of going straight on up to Francistown and then on to Maun. I was a bit apprehensive because I feared my posting had been changed but my fears were groundless. When I respectfully eased my way into the office of the Administrative Secretary, he told me the District Commissioner in Francistown whose deputy was on leave had "a bit too much hay on his fork" and had asked that I should help out for a couple of weeks. I was a bit puzzled by this because I knew there was another junior District Officer on the station but I tried to appear eager to help.

When I got to Francistown it soon became obvious to me that Norman Matthews who was the District Commissioner and who was normally a good administrator was going through a very bad patch with the bottle. He didn't like his junior assistant and for some reason was fond of me which was why he had asked for me until the deputy he trusted returned from his short leave. The appointment of the junior assistant was not confirmed after his probation period expired so perhaps Norman's judgement that he was "hopeless" was correct. Norman could never forget that he once found the poor chap eating an ice cream at his desk!

The persecuted junior had the same Christian name as me. Norman would frequently bellow for me when he wanted to tell me something. The first time this happened the junior rushed into his office gratified that he was being addressed by Christian name by his persecutor. When Norman looked up and saw who had answered his bellow he bawled out the poor chap so ferociously that he crashed into me in his retreat because I was just behind him responding to the summons.

I felt very sorry for Norman and more particularly for his wife who was very loyal and supportive. He was always in the office promptly to start the day but at about half past ten he would disappear and return about 20 minutes later. He would almost invariably bawl out the junior District Officer and then come into my office on some flimsy pretext. He took a keen interest in whatever I was doing. He never got in the way and without being patronising often made valuable and sometimes inspired suggestions about how to reply to a letter or deal with some problem. I'm afraid he wasn't much use in the afternoons and usually spent most of the time behind his closed door. But he would emerge as bright as a button shortly after five and would cart me off down to one or other of the two hotels for a cold beer. He was always treated with great respect and seemed to be genuinely popular.

He was a good raconteur and often entertained me with stories of the old days – he joined the service when I was about five years old. One tale in particular amused me greatly. When he was still a bachelor he ran a sort of mess on the station and two or three of his fellow bachelors used to eat together in his house. Norman had a very good cook who hailed from Nyasaland and, inevitably, was called Banda. The bachelors ate extremely well but Norman suspected the cook was stealing his liquor. He seemed to be over fond of sherry. So Norman set a trap.

He turned the bottle upside down and marked the level of liquor on the label. When he examined it a few days later his suspicions were confirmed – the level had dropped. As the week progressed there was always a pre-dinner check on the sherry level that had always gone down. Norman kept topping it up by peeing in it. At the end of the week Banda was called in whilst the bachelors were drinking their coffee and Norman accused him of drinking his sherry. The cook denied this but Norman produced the bottle and told him how he had personally replenished the contents. Banda confounded them all when he informed them the sherry went down because he used a little every evening to flavour their soup!

He amused me on another occasion with a story about how his District Commissioner told him one Monday morning about something that had happened the previous day. This District Commissioner's Afghan hound had startled him just before lunchtime by appearing on the verandah with a leg of mutton still dripping with gravy clenched between its jaws. He decided to go and have his lunch and leave the hound to enjoy his meal.

There was another District Officer on the station who told Norman when they were having their morning cup of tea that a joint of meat had disappeared from his kitchen the previous lunchtime. His cook had taken the joint out of the oven and put it on the table near the window while he returned to the stove to attend to the vegetables but when he looked again the meat dish was empty. He was convinced the kitchen was bewitched. Norman voiced his astonishment but he didn't shop the Afghan.

Although Norman was going through a bad spell when I was with him in Francistown he never let the side down. A few months later a caring government sent him off for treatment and after one relapse, he got over his problems, won promotion on merit and after a useful tail end to his career retired happily to the Cape.

Colonial life was characterised by a lot of hard drinking and I soon learnt how wise the ex-Tanganyika administrator who had given us lectures on the Devonshire course had been to impress upon us the drinking 'rule of three'. Of course we often had great parties and sad mornings followed happy nights but it was wise to be careful because social drinking could get out of control and solitary drinking on 'one man' stations often took its toll. Of course most of the officials never suffered more than the occasional retributive hangover but without doubt there were some prodigious drinkers.

Anyway, my spell with Norman in Francistown soon passed – I think I was of some help in a difficult period for him – and off I went to Maun which was the principal settlement and the capital of the northwest district known as Ngamiland.

I was spared the rigours of the road journey from Francistown because an air service had been introduced recently. The plane was a five-seater and the pilot, a rather curious man called Herbert Bartaune, was also a passionate hunter. He flew very low at about 100 feet so that he could indulge in game spotting. It was a great trip more so because it was the first time I had been in an aeroplane. I think Herbert was of German origin but to my knowledge nobody seemed to be curious about what he had got up to during the war or if they were they kept it to themselves. He was shaped like a gigantic pear and fitted into his seat with difficulty but he was an excellent bush pilot.

I was awestruck by my first sight of Maun with the wetlands behind it and the Thamalakane river flowing out of them. After the tawny landscape of the desert and the stark, grayish white of the vast Makgadikgadi salt pans, the glittering blue water of the river and the green-tinged channels and lagoons beyond seemed to belong to another world. Herbert Bartaune made a wide swoop around Maun to give me some idea of the hinterland (I was the only passenger) and then made a perfect landing on the dirt landing strip that served as the airport.

Alighting from the plane I was struck by a wall of heat – it was early September and beginning to warm up. But I then became aware of a quality of the air that was so unlike other parts of the country. It was not dry and brittle but had a softness that must have been caused by the presence of so much water.

Mike Williams – the squash Blue from Tshabong – met me. He was my age but my senior in service because, having been born and educated in South Africa and recruited locally, he had not been required to spend two years marking time whilst on National Service. He was the District Commissioner and I was to serve under him. He took me off to the Residency because I was to stay with him for a couple of days whilst I sorted out my bits and pieces which had preceded me by road transport.

Ngamiland

Ngamiland was a large administrative district comprising about 35,000 square miles with a population of about 40,000 of whom 200 were Europeans and the rest Africans. The ruling tribe was the Batawana but there were others – BaYei, Mbukushu, Herero and River Bushmen. The headquarters – Maun – was about 320 miles from the nearest railhead at Francistown and the connecting road was, for the most part, appalling. It was often impassable in the rains when the sand turned to mud and in the dry season the heavy sand made the going difficult. Goods transport was by heavy-duty vehicles and 20-30 hour travelling times were not unusual. The going was quicker by smaller one ton trucks but even then 12 hours was a good time. As a result Maun and the other villages which were mainly to the west and north west were a long way from what passed as civilisation in the east. I suppose it was this remoteness which accounted for the eccentricity of some of the white residents.

The Okavango River enters the district in the far north west. It originates in the highlands of Angola and is fed by the summer rains there. At its source it is a mere 200 miles or so from the Atlantic but, rather perversely, it flows away from this towards the Indian Ocean nearly 2,000 miles away to the east. But it never makes it to the sea because soon after it leaves the Caprivi Strip it is checked by a fault line and spreads out into a triangular area of about 4,000 square miles which consists of swamps, lakes and lagoons connected by braided channels. It eventually flows out of these vast wetlands and continues in a roughly south easterly direction skirting Maun and other villages until the sands of the Kalahari swallow it up.

The oddity about the wetlands is that because the summer floods of Angola take so long to reach them the waters are at their highest in the dry season and at their lowest in the wet season. In its passage through the papyrus and other reeds the water becomes crystal clear. The bird life in these wetlands is abundant and they are also home to vast herds of wild animals of almost every description – and also home to the tsetse fly. The waters are full of fish, crocodiles and hippo and the vegetation is unlike that in any other part of the country. It was a wonderful station for a young bachelor.

I much enjoyed my two and a half years in Ngamiland – so much so that I never bothered to take leave although we were allowed two weeks occasional leave a year in addition to our long leave that accrued at the rate of four days a month. It was great to work with Mike Williams. He was a first class administrator and although he was my superior officer he never pulled rank. We were both bachelors, 27 years old. We got on very well with each other and I cannot remember our having a single disagreement. We also got on very well with the local inhabitants of all races who seemed to like us and accepted our gently imposed authority.

It was not long before I realised that the district was beset by many problems. It was remote from the rest of the country and the cost of living was high because of the high cost of road transport. It was huge and like most of Bechuanaland sparsely populated. It consisted of two widely different areas. The Okavango wetlands that were about 4,000 square miles in extent and outside these, typical Kalahari sandveldt lacking surface water. There were six principal villages at almost equal intervals around the edge of the swamp area that, because of the tsetse, was unsuitable for permanent settlement. Travelling around this district was laborious because of the heavy sand and, in many places, what was known locally as black turf. When it rained this became thick and glutinous and made travelling difficult to say the least. The trucks would sink up to their axles in clinging mud and digging them out was hard work. One particularly heavy stretch of road was known as the 'Portuguese customs post' by the locals because of the time that it took to negotiate it. These black turf stretches were almost always in areas where the tsetse fly had ballooned out from the swamplands. Digging out a truck under an onslaught of tsetse was not particularly pleasant.

It was a constant battle to keep the tsetse in the wetlands where they belonged. The health problems were prodigious. Not only was malaria endemic but sleeping sickness took its toll. We lived in constant threat of the rabies that smouldered in the wildlife population. The large herds of buffalo certainly carried foot and mouth disease that periodically spilled over into the cattle herds and then the district was sealed off from the rest of the country by cordon fences that were patrolled by veterinary officials.

Schooling had been long neglected. The school buildings were hopelessly inadequate, very badly equipped and staffed by mediocre teachers. As a result the general standard of education of the inhabitants was not high. There were of course many exceptions.

One was the Regent Mrs Moremi and another the Tribal Secretary Tsheko Tsheko. The Regent was not a local but was born and educated in the Orange Free State of South Africa. By training she was a nurse. She was tiny – not much more that five feet tall – and very plump. She could put on a fine display of fierce indignation when she was crossed – on these occasions she reminded me of an angry bantam hen. But she was very bright, shrewd and strong-willed. She needed all these qualities because many of the tribal elders resented her authority – not only was she a woman but she was a foreigner to boot. Her husband when he was alive had not been much use to the tribe. He had been over fond of the bottle and he had died in a car crash when he was far from sober. He was not driving at the time but was tormenting the driver by pulling out the choke and the truck overturned at a sharp corner on a sandy road.

The Tribal Secretary (who told me how the accident happened) was with him at the time but fortunately for his wife and seven children and also for Ngamiland and Bechuanaland, he survived. Tsheko Tsheko or TT as he was usually called (but not ever by me because I respected him too much to become familiar with him) was an outstanding man. I got to know him very well because I worked closely with him in the Tribal Treasury. Later when he was Minister of Agriculture I was appointed as his Permanent Secretary. He was about the same size as Mrs Moremi but in contrast to her I never heard him raise his voice in anger and I never saw him lose his temper. He neither smoked nor drank and was always immaculately dressed either in a suit or matching bush jacket and trousers.

He was very good company and loved to hear stories about the odd behaviour of some of the locals – both white and black. He had a rich satisfying laugh – he loved a story I told him about a man who described to me a fight he had with his brother and told me his cowardly sibling kicked him in the "fillet steak". He was deeply respected by the white traders and officials but like Mrs Moremi he had a tough time with the tribesmen many of whom were very truculent.

Mike Williams and I realised early on that the development of the schools was a top priority and we started spending accumulated funds on building and equipment. There wasn't very much to go round but we did our best and we made vast improvements. We also started a determined recruiting drive to get competent staff. This was not easy because well-qualified teachers preferred being nearer the line of rail. But we gradually raised the standard – often we had to give well-qualified people who had blotted their copybook elsewhere a chance to redeem themselves and this policy worked in many cases.

Tsheko Tsheko was a great help in all of this. One of my jobs was to do a monthly audit of the Tribal Treasury books and produce a balance sheet. I often felt embarrassed checking Tsheko Tsheko's work because he knew infinitely more about bookkeeping than I did and I don't think I ever found a mistake. Often when we were going over the books we would hear the strident voice of Mrs Moremi berating someone for some misdeed and Tsheko Tsheko would look at me cock his head towards the noise and smile slightly.

Occasionally we went together on trips around the district. Once when we travelling up the eastern rim of the swamps he asked the driver to stop and pointed out a large wild fig tree to me. He told me that towards the end of the last century his grandparents fled from the Zambesi area with other members of their tribe because some warlike neighbours were persecuting them. They entered Ngamiland and a couple of miles north of the fig tree they established camp. Runners were sent to the Batawana chief asking for asylum for the fugitives and whilst he didn't trust them, he agreed to a parley with the warriors provided they attended unarmed. He appointed the shade of the fig tree as the meeting place.

It was a men-only gathering and after discussions lasting an hour or so and on a signal from the Batawana chief, his warriors retrieved their weapons from the sand where they had buried them earlier before the meeting and slaughtered the fugitives to a man. The exultant warriors wanted to go and finish off the rest of the fugitives but their chief said there had been enough killing and gathered up the old men, women and children and gave them sanctuary in his village. I asked Tsheko Tsheko if he wasn't bitter about how the Batawana had treated his people but he said he wasn't because given the chance his people would have treated the Batawana in the same way.

He also told me about a certain Captain Potts who was District Commissioner in Maun in the early 1930s. Apparently he didn't like the croaking of frogs but liked to take his sundowners on the lawn of the Residency by the side of the river. Shortly after sundown the frogs would start up. Captain Potts had two policemen stationed on the lawn behind him and when the croaking reached top pitch a raised finger from him instructed the policemen to fire a round each from their rifles over the river and into the trees on the other side. A curtain of silence fell immediately and only gradually was the chorus resumed. Tsheko Tsheko said as a little boy he would listen to the shots – usually three salvoes in all – and after the final one would know that the 'molaudi' had finished his sundowners and was about to dine.

On tour in Ngamiland

Travelling around the district was most enjoyable and the 'touring team' on hand at Maun was first class. The mode of travel was by caboose. This consisted of a five ton diesel chassis on which had been built a compartment with two bunk beds, a wardrobe and a wash basin area. Behind this compartment was a wire mesh area for carrying supplies and the touring team. The driver was a Coloured man (that is to say of mixed race) called Jack Ramsden. He was a splendid fellow – a first class driver, a superb shot and highly intelligent. He was later to be instrumental in establishing the first game conservation area in the Okavango – the Moremi Wildlife Reserve – and became a senior game warden.

The relief driver was one of the ugliest men I have ever met.

He was squat with heavy features. He was powerfully muscled and walked with his head and shoulders slightly ahead of the rest of him. He was called Kambo Kambo and was from one of the local swamp tribes. He spoke little English. He once told me – through Jack Ramsden – that his first job with Government was as a messenger between a police post on the western rim of the swamps and another about 100 miles to the north. He travelled on foot and once asked the European post commander at one of the posts for a rifle because the lions were very troublesome on his travels. He was told that no lion would attack him because he would frighten it off just by looking at it.

But Kambo was a good man and an expert at digging out trucks stuck in the mud. The sight of him bare to the waist, his black skin glistening with sweat and his muscles rippling under it as he wielded the spade always reminded me of one of Hieronymus Bosch's demons stoking the fires of hell. However, this was most unjust because in fact he was kind, willing and always helpful.

He was also a very good bush mechanic. We once came across an African driver whose truck had broken down. Apparently his carburettor had given in and he had tried to clean it – it was probably clogged with sand. When he reassembled it he couldn't get it to work again. Kambo Kambo had a go. He soon had the carburettor in pieces and I was amazed at how delicately he sorted them out with his thick, blunt fingers. He then peered at the parts for a long time and eventually said something to the driver who produced a piece of the carburettor from his pocket. Kambo's barked criticism of the unfortunate driver sent the team into hysterics and when I asked Jack to share the joke he said Kambo had told the driver that when you mend carburettors my friend there must be no 'surplus' when you have finished.

The lorry labourer was a lad of about 20 called Mapunya –

usually called Poons. He was quite tall and very slender with a loping, bobbing stride – he reminded me of a praying mantis. He spoke English after a fashion and when he was nervous he developed a stutter which was not so severe as to be disabling or embarrassing and served to increase one's affection for him – at least that was the effect it had on me. He usually stuttered when he spoke to me because he was always a bit nervous when confronted with 'authority' or so Jack Ramsden told me. I acquired a new pick-up truck and once we went out in convoy. Jack was driving and Poons was sitting in the back that was open. When we passed through a village or any settlement Poons would shout something several times in a loud voice. Jack told me he was shouting "Nylon" to indicate to the people that the truck was new! Nylon at that time was an exciting innovation in the undeveloped world.

The third member of this remarkable team was also quite a character. He was employed as a messenger/interpreter. He was called Thomas Allifeyo, a Nyasa who was useless as an interpreter because, although he was married to a local woman, his knowledge of Setswana was almost non-existent. His English was adequate for simple conversations but not for anything else. When we first met I amazed him by greeting him in Chinjanja. I had learnt the greeting pattern when I shared rooms in London with someone who was destined for Nyasaland as a District Officer.

Thomas owed his employment to the fact that he was a splendid cook. He had been recruited by Norman Matthews when he was District Commissioner at Maun. To be served superb meals with breakfasts complete with toast and marmalade in the bush was a very satisfying experience. He was also a competent barber and usually charged 6d for a haircut but he didn't charge Mike Williams or me. He always had his scissors and trimmer with him and often gave me a trim whilst the others were setting up the evening camp. I remember well that Thomas was cutting my hair whilst I listened to the news of Sputnik on the saucepan wireless I had with me. Sometimes when we called at a trading store our departure was delayed whilst Thomas gave the trader a haircut.

Travelling around this huge district and being looked after by this splendid team was like being on an expensive safari. Poons was in charge of the ancient old Greener shotgun and he always bagged guinea fowl or duck and sometimes both on our trips and Thomas cooked them superbly in the large black three-legged pot. He also made bread in a black flat-bottomed pot. He would make a slight hole in the ground, fill it with hot coals, put the pot on these and then heap more coals all around and on the lid to form a sort of oven. We always carried fishing rods and when we camped near water we would catch bream which were delicious to eat. However, we usually avoided camping near water because the mosquitoes bred there and the Ngamiland variety were plump and savage. I often thought life was unfair – we were bitten by tsetse during the day and when the sun went down and the tsetse went to bed the mosquitoes took over.

I remember the first time I visited the Tsodilo Hills on one of our trips. These are in the far north west of the district up towards the Caprivi Strip border. This small group of kopjes was about 40 miles from what passed as the main road but fairly easy to approach along an easily visible bush track. We camped under a huge wild fig tree and explored the various rock faces and caves many of which are illuminated with outstanding Bushman paintings.

I was amused to recall that in one of his books Laurens van der Post claimed that he was the first white man to look upon this rock art and that he virtually discovered the Hills. In fact the paintings and the Hills were a well-known if rather remote tourist attraction long before van der Post laid eyes on them and I understand he was actually guided there by a District Officer called Ernest Midgley who was stationed in the area at that time. Another District Officer called Captain Stigand visited the Hills regularly in the early 1930s whilst he was stationed at Maun because he was a keen rock climber. About 30 years before this a German explorer called Siegfried Passarge visited them and took photographs of several of the paintings for illustrations in his book about the Kalahari Bushmen.

Laurens van der Post also claimed the hills were haunted and because one member of his party shot a steenbok near the track to them, he had to placate the Spirits of Tsodilo by writing a letter to them. This he claimed did the trick because their campfire began to burn brightly and the string of little accidents dried up. He didn't say what language he used. However, we didn't have to do any placating even though Poons shot some guinea fowl on the way there and we had a wonderful two days exploring the caves and soaking up the lonely beauty of the Hills especially at sunrise and sunset. The caboose team was highly amused when I recounted van der Post's fanciful stories.

I subsequently visited the Hills many times but on one occasion a police superintendent, Ted Warren – who was the OC of the district and stationed in Maun – accompanied me. He was inspecting the various police posts and at one of them, Tsau, there were some prisoners awaiting trial and he was going to be the prosecutor before me in my capacity as magistrate.

We set off from Tsodilo very early. It was just getting light – the time the Batswana describe very poetically as "dinako tsa dikgomo" which means "the horns of the cattle" because the light is just strong enough to pick out the horns of the cattle when they are moving through the bush grazing. We set off early because we were due in court in the middle of the morning. A couple of miles or so outside Tsau we stopped and ate one of Thomas' superb breakfasts. We then washed and shaved. I changed into a crisply starched bush jacket and long khaki trousers. Ted Warren changed into his number one uniform complete with highly polished Sam Browne and gleaming shoes. We were just about to set off when we heard the noise of vehicles approaching and we waited until they drew alongside.

They turned out to be two open jeeps containing half a dozen or so American tourists who were being taken to Tsodilo by a local safari operator cum crocodile hunter called John Seaman whom I knew well. They were all very grubby – caked in dust and mostly unshaven. John, who I could see was enjoying himself hugely, introduced us to them by name and title, making us sound very important.

The Americans were quite simply awestruck. One of them asked if we were always so immaculately turned out when we travelled in the bush and I'm afraid we left him with the impression that we were and this was all part of 'keeping the flag flying'. John, Jack and the rest of the caboose team much enjoyed the mild deception. The evening crowd in Riley's hotel also enjoyed John Seaman's re-enactment of the scene when he put on a performance there later in the week.

Ngamiland places and people

Tsau was a sprawling, untidy sort of village. A corporal and four troopers manned the police post and there was a school and a couple of trading stores but despite this the village had a strange air of impermanence. I think this was because it was situated right on the edge of tsetse country and the Tsetse Fly Control Department waged a constant battle to contain the fly by bush clearing and selective spraying. Sometimes it looked as though they were losing.

George Kyriacou, a trader at Tsau, was usually known as 'Dirty George'. I was told that this was really his uncle's sobriquet that George had inherited when his uncle died. I liked George despite the fact that he was a bit of an old rogue. He always treated me with profound respect and although I was very much younger than he was, never ever addressed me by my given name. He was most hospitable and whenever I stayed in Tsau overnight at the police camp in the guest rondavel, hardly had I arrived when a messenger would appear with an invitation from George to go and have supper with him. Supper was usually a boisterous affair with lots to drink.

He told me about a young doctor who committed suicide in Tsau. He was a government doctor and I believe he was very upset because he had got a young African woman with child – in those days this was a serious disgrace when a senior government official was involved. I think the reasoning was that it destroyed the trust that had to exist between the governed and governors. The young doctor was so upset that he blew his brains out in the guest rondavel down in the police lines. George heard the shot when he was sitting on his verandah just prior to turning in and was very uneasy. His fears were confirmed when the police corporal, who had no motor transport, came to seek assistance. George said the young man's brains were hanging from the rafters. This made me a bit uneasy because I was due to sleep in the same rondavel that night.

Later he repeated this story in the bar of the Maun hotel whilst we were waiting to go in to dinner. One of our party was a rather twittery woman and she almost had hysterics when George came to the bit about the brains. Later when we trooped in to dinner, she had a more serious attack of hysterics because when she read the menu she saw that one of the courses was brains on toast. George sat back looking quite pleased with himself. I am sure he had seen the menu beforehand and had set the woman up.

One of the Ngamiland traders was once involved in an incident which was discussed at length in Riley's Hotel. This trader's wife was very beautiful and much younger than her husband. Several of the trader's relatives worked in or around the store and the chief assistant was a young man in his early twenties. He was quite handsome and although a little on the plump side, very presentable. He was the trader's nephew and he treated the young man rather like a son but in a very authoritarian manner.

The trader became very suspicious that his young assistant was more than usually close to his 'auntie' and from his seat behind the counter in the store he observed the goings on with his great hooded eyes but said nothing. He frequently made trips to Bulawayo where he had business connections and when he did he was usually away for two or three weeks. He set off one afternoon ostensibly bound for Bulawayo but a few miles out of the village he camped and waited. About a couple of hours after sundown he returned to the village and, parking his truck a few hundred yards from his compound, approached his house stealthily on foot. He saw a light burning in his bedroom and, on peering through the window, saw vivid and vigorous confirmation of his suspicions.

With a Potiphar-like roar he burst through the door and the naked young assistant disappeared through the window into the African night. The rest of the clan, awakened by the trader's loudly proclaimed fury and his wife's entreaties for mercy, crowded in and stopped the beating. They gradually calmed the old man down and got him installed in an easy chair in the sitting room and poured him a large brandy.

After a while the young seducer, realising that he would somehow have to make his peace with his uncle and no doubt because his plump body was being tormented by mosquitoes, returned to the house and being assured that the old man had calmed down, approached him on his knees. The young Lothario must have been a sadly comical sight because he had girded his naked loins with an empty flour sack. Kneeling in front of his uncle who was sitting with his chin on his chest and a cigarette dangling from his lips, the young lover begged for forgiveness saying what a noble man his uncle was and how he owed everything to him. He got rather carried away and declared that the trader was his "beloved father" which had the opposite of the intended effect because it served to rekindle the older man's rage. He leapt to his feet and began kicking the young man because he had been "f***ing his own mother".

However they patched things up and when the young wife's black eye and the nephew's bruises and mosquito bites faded away life seemed to return to what passed as normal at the trading station.

Some of the other traders in the district were equally colour-ful characters. One couple – the Wrights – ran a store at a village called Nokaneng that, like Tsau, was on the rim of the wetlands and under constant threat from the fly. Mrs Wright operated a radio and kept in touch with Maun via the police network. She told me that once her radio was out of order at a time when the Chief Tsetse Fly Control Officer was camping in the village devising means of pushing the fly back. His routine was to go out very early in the morning and do whatever he had to do before returning about ten for a late breakfast. One morning when he returned to his camp instead of staying for breakfast he rushed to his truck and left for Maun without saying anything to his staff who were much puzzled by his odd behaviour.

When radio communications were restored three or four days later Mrs Wright was able to unravel the mystery of the disappearing Chief Tsetse Fly Control Officer. When he had returned to camp he went into the cooking enclosure to grab a snack because he was hungry but as he was approaching the gap in the enclosure a dog, foaming at the mouth, dashed out, bit him in the leg and disappeared into the bush. Convinced he had been bitten by a rabid dog he took off immediately for Maun hospital.

However, when Mrs Wright investigated the incident she discovered the dog was not rabid but was feeding puppies and being half starved had been gobbling maize meal porridge from one of the iron cooking pots when she had been disturbed. She had fled with a mouthful of porridge. When Mrs Wright got on the radio she was able to halt the course of very painful injections that were being administered to the tsetse fly man.

Mrs Wright also told me about a man who stayed with them for a few days before setting off with African guides and two mokoros (dug out canoes) to go hunting in the wetlands. A couple of weeks later he was brought back in a makeshift litter carried by the guides – he was desperately ill – far too ill to make it to the Maun hospital about 120 miles away. Mrs Wright knew he had blackwater fever because Andrew her husband had had it twice and – miraculously – had survived. She had nursed him.

She firmly believed that one of the essentials in the caring process was not to give the patient any solid food whatsoever and after a week under her care the sick man began to show signs of recovery. One morning she went to collect eggs from the hen run and when she returned was horrified to see the Herero woman servant feeding the patient with bread and milk. She dashed the bowl from the woman's hand who explained tearfully that the man had woken and asked for food because he was very hungry. Later that afternoon the man lapsed into a coma and

Mrs Wright told the servant he would not last much longer and she would keep vigil throughout the night. The poor servant said she would keep her company

Long after midnight Mrs Wright was sitting knitting and listening to the stertorous breathing of the patient. The Herero was sitting on the floor at the foot of the bed with her head covered in a blanket that she was using as a shawl and every now and then moaning her distress. Suddenly the breathing stopped and Mrs Wright murmured to the Herero (in her language) that she was afraid he had gone. She put down her knitting and with her back to the foot of the bed bent down to listen for a heartbeat with her good ear. She could detect no sounds of life but suddenly the 'corpse' let out a piercing scream and she started back. When she looked at the foot of the bed she saw that the Herero had the patient's big toe clenched between her strong white teeth and had obviously bitten hard down on him. The patient recovered – amazingly – and Mrs Wright learnt that it was common practice amongst the Herero to do the big toe test just to make sure that death had arrived.

Mrs Wright had two sons and a daughter. The youngest son was called Dougie and we engaged him on a temporary task of supervising a gang of labourers who were attempting to clear a channel in the reed beds to improve the flow of water down the western edge of the swamps. Although Dougie was only 16 or 17 years old at the time he knew the area intimately and was able to guide the clearing operations. One day when the gang was busy clearing the reeds a lion paid them a visit and young Dougie decided to have a crack at it. He hit it in mid charge and wounded it very badly but it kept on coming and bowling him over gave him a severe mauling before succumbing to its wound. In the meantime the labourers had panicked and leapt into the stream. Jack Ramsden who reported all this to me said the labourers behaved like sitatunga (water kudu) which when they want to hide submerge themselves in the water with only their mouth and nostrils showing. However, being a fit young fellow Dougie soon recovered and went on to become a very fine white hunter before transferring to the non-hunting safari business.

Riley's Hotel

The drinking establishment in Maun was known to everyone as Riley's Hotel because that was the name of the first owner. He had the rather grand name of Harold Beauchamp Riley (I think he was born in Mauritius) and had lived in Maun for most of his life beside the river that flowed past his house but he had never learned to swim. In 1954 there were heavy rains. The river came down in flood and washed away the road bridge into Maun from Francistown. Harry Riley also owned the transport service between Maun and Francistown and one of his trucks and its passengers was marooned on the wrong side of the river at the bridge site. Harry, very nobly, went to help ferry the passengers and their goods across the swollen river and whilst ferrying across a family complete with iron bedstead, the boat capsized. Harry became entangled in the ironwork of the bed and was swept away.

Chobo Weskob, a local trader, told me that Harry Riley had been a great practical joker. He was fond of playing poker as was Chobo and some of the Greek traders – in particular Butch Francopoulus the local butcher. Harry arranged a poker school from time to time on the verandah of the hotel. Chobo said they were playing the cards one evening when Harry excused himself for a few moments. Whilst he was away from the table suddenly the whole place was brilliantly lit up. There was no electric light in Maun in those days so the card players were astounded at the brightness. Harry returned to the table and picked up his hand to resume playing and ignored the surprised chatter of the other players. Eventually unable to restrain his mirth any longer he took the players to a shed adjacent to the verandah where a burly African was vigorously pedalling a bicycle mounted on blocks and providing the verandah light by a dynamo. Chobo said the sweat was cascading from the end of his nose in a steady stream. He was relieved of his task and the players returned to the oil lamps.

Because of the laws governing the consumption of alcohol in those days the hotel was more like a club for white men. For many years Riley's Hotel was the only hotel in the country on tribal territory. All the others were on land outside tribal boundaries. The privilege afforded to Rileys was perhaps because of the remoteness of Maun from the line of rail and also because the chief had enthusiastically supported the application for a licence. Ironically it was white man's liquor which lead to the early death of this same chief, as has been recounted.

Social life for the whites in Maun centred round Riley's hotel. Every Friday there was a film show in the lounge – Uncle Tom Kays operated the projector. Most people turned up regularly and many paid for their tickets two or three months in advance. I never understood why they did because there were no reserved seats. There were also frequent bingo sessions and dances. The New Year party started in the early evening and lasted until sun up and the drinks were on the house. Whenever a new official arrived a welcome party was held for him or her and departures were also marked in a similar way.

When I first visited Riley's I was struck by the curiously constructed pathway from the car park to the verandah because at first I couldn't make out what materials had been used in its construction. Then I saw that the curved metal strips separating the gravelly parts of the path were broken truck spring blades. This seemed symbolic of the remoteness of Maun from the railhead and the difficulty experienced in negotiating the distance. Over a drink in the bar, the government doctor told me he was once called out to one of Riley's trucks that had interrupted its journey from Francistown and had stopped a mile or so away from Maun because one of the passengers was giving birth. When he admonished the woman for undertaking a journey in her condition she told him that when she boarded the truck in Francistown she had not been pregnant. I am sure the people in the bar had heard the story many times before but they all laughed – I think they were making me feel at home.

There were about 60 adult white people living in Maun in the mid-50s and a fair proportion congregated in Riley's most evenings. They were an interesting and often amusing bunch. They were very shrewd observers of human behaviour. Anyone who put on airs was mercilessly dissected and exposed as a fraud. Nothing missed their notice – the married woman who left the bar shortly after a man who was not her husband had departed and returned a short while later with dead leaves tangled in her hair did not escape their scrutiny.

The conversation usually revolved about local matters of concern – the price of immature cattle that were sold to Northern Rhodesia or the price of bonemeal were often discussed. Occasionally some new and salacious topic swam into their ken and this was discussed in detail – who was present at a moonlight skinny dip at Matlapaneng bridge, which husband in the Government Camp was being cuckolded – stories like these which were embroidered with each telling kept the bar going whenever the incidents were recalled by someone bored with bonemeal or calves.

Not many tourists came through in those days because access by road was difficult and the air service was in its very early stages of development. One person who made it was Mike

Hoare who later became infamous as a mercenary in the Congo and after that in the Seychelles.

When he visited Maun however he seemed harmless enough and was on holiday from his car dealing business in Durban. His visit coincided with our celebration of the Queen's Birthday and I invited him to the drinks party that followed the parade. He arrived early and was chatting to me whilst we were waiting for the other guests to arrive. He asked me what I thought about the bar tender at Riley's who was a new arrival called MacGibbon. I said we all thought him an odd fish. His wife was obviously very much older than he was but nobody held that against him. The main reason nobody liked him much was that he was an inveterate liar. For instance he told us shortly after his arrival that his wife was French. We were inclined to believe this at first because her English was not very good but we discovered later that she was actually Afrikaans and came from Parys in the Orange Free State and not from Paris!

Mike Hoare then told me that the last time he had seen MacGibbon he was sporting a very short haircut and was in prison garb because he was doing time in Pretoria Gaol. He had obtained a car fraudulently from Hoare who was trying to get his money back. When Hoare walked into the bar at Riley's hotel seeking accommodation, MacGibbon looked startled and called out to his elderly wife whom he called 'Cookie' that they had been discovered. This story interested me because I knew that when MacGibbon filled in his immigration papers, which people coming to live permanently in the country had to do, he must have declared that he had no previous criminal convictions otherwise he would not have been issued with a residence permit.

I reported this conversation to the police inspector when he arrived for the party. He later found out from the South African Police that MacGibbon had recently been released from Pretoria

Gaol after serving a sentence for embezzlement and that he had 18 other previous criminal convictions including four for bigamy. We didn't bother to enquire whether his latest partner was his legal wife but we suspected that she wasn't and had some pathetic savings stashed away which MacGibbon was after. The regulars in the bar felt very sorry for her but they were both shipped out on one of Riley's seven ton diesel trucks.

The Kays family

One of the old settler families in Maun was the Kays. Uncle Tom, as he was invariably addressed by everyone who knew him, was a Londoner and had arrived in Maun in the 1920s. Shortly after he arrived he began courting Rosie Brierley, the daughter of a police sergeant who was stationed at Tsau, about 150 miles away. He used to visit her on his Red Indian motor bike. He must have been quite a gallant. Eventually Tom and Rosie married and settled in Maun. Rosie's sister Mary married Chobo Weskob.

When I knew the Kays, Uncle Tom was a mechanic and worked in Riley's garage, next to Riley's hotel. He and Auntie Rosie lived in a house on the banks of the Thamalakane River with their two adult sons and their married daughter lived close by. Auntie Rosie's aged mother – who was Mom to her and Uncle Tom but Granny to everyone else – was also part of the household. She was a bit of an old crone and I suspect had been quite a tartar when she was younger. Her police sergeant husband abandoned her and I think that was when she came to live with the Kays. We could always get a rise out of her by saying something in praise of the police. Her invariable response was "All policemen are bastards" and if Auntie Rosie was within earshot she would chortle in embarrassment.

In the early days before a hotel was opened in Maun, liquor was brought in from the line of rail by ox wagon. This journey took several weeks and liquor shortages were quite common when the wagon was held up for one reason or another. Chobo Weskob told me that to cope during these shortages Granny invented a sort of desperation cocktail that she made out of any dregs of commercial liquor she could scrounge from around the village plus other ingredients such as dried fruit and sugar. She called it Bull Pup and Chobo said you had to be careful to open your mouth as soon as you swallowed it to prevent it blowing the top of your head off.

Chobo also told me that Uncle Tom once developed ear trouble and a wily Seventh Day Adventist missionary doctor persuaded him that the best cure was total abstinence so he banned liquor from the house. Granny stayed in business by setting up a still near a wild fig tree on the banks of the Thamalakane a short distance from the house.

The Kays had two sons. Ronny was a steady person who was the business brains of the family. Kenny the younger one was wild even by Maun standards. Someone told me that once when they were out hunting they came across a large herd of zebra. Kenny got on the back of the open truck and telling a passenger who was a youngster barely into his teens to drive alongside the herd, succeeded in straddling one of the animals for a brief but hair-raising ride.

One Sunday the police inspector and I had been out duck shooting and when we were returning to Maun in the late afternoon we came across some very fresh elephant dung. We had some sacks with us and we carefully transferred some of the dung to the back of the truck and took it with us to Maun. When we arrived at the hotel it was dark and we carefully arranged the dung alongside the path to the bar and then went in for a drink.

It worked like a charm. Kenny finished his beer and went outside to answer nature's call. He shot back into the bar seconds later with his eyes popping out of his head because there were "elephants all round the hotel".

The Kay's daughter lived close by with her husband who had been a government Livestock Officer but retired from the service after his marriage to help the Kay boys run the family trading store in the village. He was a highly intelligent person but like most of the young white males in Maun in those days a bit on the wild side. There was a huge fig tree in what passed as the hotel car park and whenever he was short of brake power which seemed to be quite often he used to coast up to it very gently in his truck and come to rest against it.

He much enjoyed playing a rough South African game called Bok Bok on the stoep (verandah) of Riley's hotel. This consisted of two teams (all men) one crouched with heads tucked under the arm of the man in front to form a sort of snake. The others bunched at a distance. They then charged down individually and, by leaping high in the air and landing on an exposed back with terrific force one after the other, sought to bring the opposing side to its collective knees through the weakness of the unfortunate individual who had been selected as the target for aerial bombardment. It was a savage game and one visiting, rather wimpish, Government official who was persuaded to join in, retired with what was later diagnosed as several cracked ribs.

Lionel Palmer – for that was the wild man's name, was also a splendid shot. So were the Kays boys. They bought cattle from the villagers at their trading store and they had learned to shoot straight to protect them from lions when they trekked them north through wild country to sell them in Northern Rhodesia. The only way they could get them across the wide, swiftly flowing Chobe/Zambezi Rivers' confluence was to swim them over in batches tethered four a side to a motorised barge. Whilst doing so they had to try and protect them from crocodiles which swarmed to snatch a meal when crossing was in progress. Invariably there were cattle casualties because it is very difficult to keep hungry crocodiles at bay when they are swarming in the water in numbers.

The Kays were spectacularly hospitable. Their house by the river was a typical 'colonial style' bungalow with a corrugated iron roof and a wrap round stoep. It was very simply furnished. It looked as though it had been recently vacated and the departing owners had left behind various bits and pieces of furniture which were of little value. But whatever it lacked in elegance was more than compensated by the generous hospitality of the Kays. Hardly a week passed without a party at their house. Uncle Tom was usually sitting in a shabby but comfortable sofa in the corner of the stoep reading a paperback thriller. He always seemed to be part of the fun although he never actually joined in. Auntie Rosie used to make sure he wasn't neglected. It was obvious that they adored each other.

Granny loved these parties. She loved her gin. I am sure she preferred it to her Bull Pup cocktail. Before any party got going Granny would ensure that her supplies didn't run out by stashing tots of gin around the house – on the tops of cupboards, behind curtains and so on.

On one occasion, a police inspector and his wife had brought their four year old boy to the party and put him down to sleep on one of the beds. We were startled later by terrified screams from the bedroom and the mother and father made a panic-stricken rush to the source of the noise. Little Jamie had been asleep on a double bed pushed against the wall under a window. The room was dimly lit by the paraffin lamps on the side stoep and he had been awakened by Granny straddling him whilst groping for the drink she had hidden on the windowsill. He told his mother later that he thought she was the wicked witch from Snow White.

Most weekends the Kays would take half a dozen or more of us out into the bush to shoot duck and guinea fowl and fish for bream. The Kays boys and Lionel Palmer knew the area intimately. Ken and Ronny had hunted over it since their school days and knew every track, island and lagoon in the huge wetland area which teemed with wild life. Most of us had pick-up trucks and the Kays would bring a five ton diesel loaded with a boat and outboard motor. We worked Saturday mornings in those days so we would set off after lunch and return late on Sunday evening. When we arrived at the chosen campsite Uncle Tom would quickly organise a camp bed in the shade and settle down with his paperback. Granny sometimes joined us on these jaunts but as tough as she was she often stayed at home because she found them tiring which was not surprising seeing she was in her late seventies.

When I set up my camp bed on one of these outings I discovered I had left my mosquito net behind. We were camping on the Botletle river near a largish village called Chanoga. The fishing was excellent on this stretch of the river but the campsite was thick with mosquitoes and they bit like bulldogs. There must have been a large pool of infected blood in the nearby village and about ten days later I paid the penalty for forgetting my mosquito net. I woke up with a throbbing headache and knew I had malaria. At first the doctor dismissed my complaint as a hangover but after I had protested loudly that this could not be after several drink-free evenings, he took a blood slide and sure enough the little bars in my blood showed up under the microscope. Even with all the wonders of modern medicine available it took me two or three weeks to recover. This really brought home to me how hard life must be for those people living in these mosquito-infested areas with little access to medical help.

More Maun people

Many of the traders in Maun had lived in Ngamiland since the early 1930s and their children had been born there. The old timers had many tales to tell. Chobo Weskob was one of them and he was a most interesting man. Chobo was the nickname given to him by the local Africans – I was told it had something to do with pounding corn in the heavy ironwood mortars with long handled wooden pestles. Presumably the connection was that Chobo was a hard-bargaining businessman.

In the early 1930s he worked as a shop assistant in the Francistown area and was paid £4 a month. The owner of the store, Jimmy Haskins senior, accused him of theft and dismissed him so Chobo decided to try his luck at acting in Hollywood. I interrupted his story to ask where he got the money from for the journey to Hollywood and was told to mind my own business.

On his way to Hollywood he stopped off in Johannesburg and got a job as an extra in a film that was being made about the Zulu wars. He and other white extras were cast as British soldiers fending off a Zulu attack. They were armed with ancient rifles and blank cartridges while the 'Zulus' (who in real life were mine labourers) were armed with rubber assegais and knobkerries. After a few rehearsals of the charge, the 'soldiers' tiring of how tame it was, put gravel in the barrels of their rifles. Their repulse of the enemy was too realistic for the 'Zulus' and what amounted to a pitched battle ensued. However, Chobo survived and made his way to Hollywood but never made it to the screen so he returned to Africa. I think he would have made a fine actor but had his ambitions been realised Ngamiland would have lost one of its characters.

When he started trading on his own account he had a hawker's licence and visited villages and outlying settlements by ox wagon in which he carried a range of goods for sale. He told me once when he visited a tiny, isolated settlement it was deserted. When he was rummaging around the huts looking for signs of life or reasons for the sudden departure of the people he came across the largely decomposed body of a man who had been tied to a tree with a trek chain. He said there were several corpses of dogs in the area. When he caught up with the people some days later they told him the dead man had been bitten by a rabid dog and became sick so they tied him to a tree and fled. He had developed hydrophobia. They could not have saved him from this incurable disease and as he was a menace to those around him they had taken the most sensible course of action.

One District Commissioner acquired a baboon when stationed in Maun. He called it Bimbo and kept the animal chained to a post on his verandah. He was a bachelor and shared his evening sundowner time with his pet and gave it the occasional sip of brandy that the baboon much enjoyed. Chobo said he once needed to see the DC on business and called on him without notice at about eight o'clock in the evening. He had had a few and so had Bimbo. Chobo said the DC looked just like Bimbo and Bimbo just like the DC. Later I discovered a grave under the rubber hedge in the Residency garden where the poor animal – Bimbo I mean – had been laid to rest.

Marthinus Drotsky was an interesting character. His father had been one of the very early settlers in the European farming block south of Ngamiland but didn't make much of a success of farming, although he did discover some spectacular limestone caves on the border with South West Africa. Marthinus didn't have regular employment and took on odd jobs whenever they were offered to him – trekking a mob of cattle to the line of rail, fence duties during a foot and mouth outbreak and dog control during a rabies scare, for instance. He smoked a coarse leaf tobacco in a Sherlock Holmes pipe and always wore a khaki shirt and trousers and a very grubby pith helmet. I don't think I ever saw him uncovered and he took his pipe out only to eat or drink. He even danced at the hotel hops with both items – pipe and helmet – in place.

His wife was a professional mourner and would pitch up at the graveside service whenever there was a funeral of a white person whether the deceased was known to her or not. Her daughter who was in her late teens usually accompanied her. They were both clad from head to foot in black and brandished tiny white handkerchiefs. As soon as mother and daughter disembarked from the family truck at the cemetery gate they would start keening and would keep this up throughout the service modulating it only when the preacher was intoning his bits. I think they enjoyed funerals immensely.

A team of American entomologists was once visiting the area on a research project and the leader asked me for a guide because they were intending to visit trackless areas. I asked Marthinus if he would accompany them because he knew the district intimately and he agreed to go along. When they returned the leader came to say goodbye and thank me for my help. He said Marthinus had proved to be an excellent guide but he was totally fascinated by him. He never saw him without his pith helmet and was convinced he slept in it. He rarely saw him without his pipe.

He told me that early one morning he was sitting in a camp chair on one side of the fire surreptitiously studying Marthinus who was squatting facing him on the other side. Suddenly Marthinus lifted his head in amazement and with his gaze fixed firmly over the American's shoulder fumbled his pipe out of his mouth. When the American turned to see what had made such an impression on Marthinus he was amazed to come face to face with a hippopotamus only about 20 yards away – particularly amazed because they were about 50 miles or so distant from water.

Mrs Drotsky later eloped with Willie Loubscher. He was a mechanic at Riley's garage and lodged with the Drotsky's. Willie was a skinny little runt of a man in his late twenties or early thirties and we all thought he was after the Drotsky daughter. He wasn't much to look at and had false teeth that he rarely wore because they were ill-fitting and hurt his gums. He wore them on social occasions but usually faced the world toothless. The eloping couple left early one morning in Willie's seven ton diesel truck bound for Swakopmund in South West Africa. I often wondered whether Willie wore his teeth on the journey or whether they were in his overall pocket. Sadly Marthinus later committed suicide but not, or so I was told, because his wife had left him.

I used to visit occasionally a man called Piet Engelbrecht who was employed by the veterinary department to maintain a section of one of the disease control fences. He lived in a desolate place and his accommodation consisted of a couple of cottage tents. I had no particular business with him but made the occasional social call if I happened to be passing close to his camp. He was always pleased to see me – he couldn't have had many visitors and when I visited him he usually helped himself liberally to my whisky.

The first time I visited him I was introduced to his wife – she was in her mid teens - about a third of Engelbrecht's age – and was giving suck to a rather lusty child. She had a cigarette dangling from her lips and from time to time would brush ash from the baby's face. Engelbrecht was enjoying a sundowner and invited me to join him knowing full well that I would make a contribution. He was nibbling something from a plate in front of him. He offered the plate to me and I gingerly took a small morsel and popped it in my mouth. When I bit it I spat it out immediately because it was a red-hot chilli. He was eating them as though they were smarties.

Engelbrecht had a baboon as a pet. He called it Apie and it was on a chain tethered to a nearby tree watching the goings on in camp bobbing its head up and down and swaying its body from side to side from a sitting position. When Mrs Engelbrecht finished feeding her baby she put it in a pram just out of reach of the baboon and stuck a bottle of orange juice in the baby's mouth. The baboon was bobbing and weaving and rocking to and fro in great excitement. The baby, who couldn't have been hungry, threw its bottle out of the pram and it sailed through the air to land in the sand in baboon territory. The animal grabbed it and started to suck the teat ecstatically. Mrs Engelbrecht noticed and leaping up with a loud shriek of "Apie!", grabbed the bottle, boxed the baboon's ears and without wiping it shoved the teat back in the baby's mouth. This happened once more so she moved the pram out of range. I thought at the time that the baby would probably grow up into a strong boy with guaranteed immunity against all harmful bacteria.

There was another fence foreman whom I used to visit from time to time. He was called Wally Stenson and must have been in his sixties. He had huge ears but was very deaf and one had to shout hard when conversing with him. During one of these shouted conversations he told me that he had been one of Baden Powell's original boy scouts in Mafikeng during the siege and I believe he was telling the truth. He enjoyed a drink and he much enjoyed my visits because I went prepared with a bottle of brandy in my brief case. Wally's wife used to ration his drinks and kept the bottle locked up so when she was in the kitchen preparing the food I would replenish the rather mean tot she had poured for Wally and he would knock it back – after two or three of these he was in fine form. Once on looking out of the window I asked him what all those rows of plants were in a fenced off area behind his house. He told me they were garlic and when I remarked (or rather shouted) that he and his wife must be rather fond of it he told me that actually they couldn't stand the stuff but it was the only vegetable that would grow there!

Jock Allan and friends

The police inspector whose son had been terrified by Granny Brierley at the Kays' house was called Jock Allan and he was a most engaging character. He was a marvellous storyteller and I do believe most of his tales were true. His wife confirmed this.

One of his tales concerned a slow-witted constable. Jock and his wife had both served in the Edinburgh police. He told us that when he was a constable the district was enlarged and a little village came within the new boundaries. The village constable was not bright but as he was nearing retirement it was decided to give him the undemanding duty of guard at the Leith dockyard gates. Someone approached him one day and asked where the urinal was. He replied that if the enquirer told him the colour of the funnel he would point it out.

Jock used to keep the Maun bar crowd entertained with equally strange tales. He was an astute observer of human nature and this made him a first rate policeman. He was very intelligent and well read but he had little formal education. He must have made a very good impression at his interview because normally a good secondary education was required for admission to the Bechuanaland Protectorate Police.

One of the hotel residents was a great favourite with Jock. She was in her mid fiftes and was Russian by birth. Her name was Sasha. Her father had been a rich kulak and when she was a young woman she had been forced to flee during the Russian revolution and became separated from the rest of her family whom she presumed simply perished. Somehow she landed up in China where she met and married Sydney Lorraine-Drew who was employed in a local customs service somewhere on the Yangtse. After much wandering they eventually landed up in Maun where Chobo Weskob employed Sydney as a bookkeeper. They lived permanently in the hotel.

Sasha was on the small side and was rather stout but she must have been a cracker when she was younger. She spoke English with a thick accent and she enjoyed a drink and company. Sydney was a slight, academic looking fellow and was very nearly a teetotaller. Sasha used to love to establish herself on a stool at the bar and enjoy the company. She had a good singing voice – a rich contralto – and from time to time Jock would get her going after she had downed a few gins. He would ask her to sing him a song from the old days and she would sing Russian folk songs.

They were very beautiful and melancholy and she sang with great feeling, her eyes behind her large spectacles brimming over with tears. After two or three songs Sydney would appear and she would greet him very affectionately calling him "my darlink". He would lead her off to their room. Poor people – they were so gentle and pleasant and must have had a very hard life. Sydney died in the late 1960s leaving poor Sasha almost destitute but John van Riet Lowe, who had known her when he was stationed at Maun as District Commissioner managed to get her fixed up in a council flat at Ruislip complete with television and a small pension from the State.

Jock seemed to be a magnet for humorous happenings. He came into my office one morning to show me a letter which he had almost signed without reading it through. It was to the Commissioner of Police who was also Chief Immigration Officer and concerned an application for a passport from the veterinary officer who was called Johannes Fuchs Fick. A police constable who acted as a clerk had typed it, using one finger I expect, from a draft written by Jock whose handwriting was appalling. The subject matter as typed by the constable was stated to be an application for a passport from 'Johannes Fuck Fick alias Jick'.

On another occasion the teacher wife of one of my clerks came to see me. They were being transferred to another station and she wanted to resume teaching after her baby was born – she was heavily pregnant – and wanted a reference from me. She was an excellent teacher and I was taking some time to write a good testimonial for her while she sat and waited in the office armchair knitting some item of baby's clothing. I looked up in response to a gentle tapping on the open door and there was Jock who saluted me in a rather avuncular manner and, bursting with mirth, deferentially begged my pardon for interrupting such a charming domestic scene and asked whether I would be free at 11 to preside in court.

He got into a scrape once when the High Commissioner and his lady complete with entourage paid a fleeting visit to Maun. They were on their way to Kasane in the north by chartered aeroplane and stopped at Maun to refuel and have lunch. The VIPs went to have lunch at the Residency and the crew, chaperoned by Jock, went to Riley's Hotel. Whilst they were lunching he had quite a few drinks at the bar. He got them back to the landing strip in good time and tucked his truck well out of the way – or so he thought. The hot sun was getting to him and he was finding it difficult to stand unsupported so he propped himself up with his back against the police truck whilst the police driver, sensing all was not well, made himself scarce.

The official party arrived and after disembarking from the cars made its way to the waiting aeroplane. Jock thought he had got away with it. He was horrified when the High Commissioner's lady, whilst turning her head to speak to someone, spotted him standing against, or rather propped up by, the truck and started walking towards him. She had met him on a previous occasion and had discovered that they both hailed from the same village in Scotland. She was anxious to greet him. Jock drew himself up to the salute as she approached but was so much in liquor that he could not trust himself to speak. So he remained silently at the salute, smiling stiffly and foolishly, until the Private Secretary, Stephen Henn, noticed that Jock was in no fit state for intelligent chit-chat and ushered the High Commissioner's lady to the aircraft. I think the Commissioner of Police issued a reprimand.

The police acted as prosecutors in those days and Jock was excellent in court. He was not vindictive and never attempted to secure a conviction at any cost. He always tried to make the court aware of all aspects of the case before it. Once he was prosecuting a man of about 50 who was accused of a very serious assault on his adult son who I think was a simpleton. He had clouted him behind the ear with a heavy hoe and cracked his skull so severely that spinal fluid had leaked out. The doctor was amazed that the lad had survived.

The accused was certainly guilty but before I passed sentence Jock asked whether he could address the court. He briefly highlighted what had happened. The accused had been hoeing his agricultural plot about 4 miles away from his kraal, and his simple son was helping him. When the father discovered he had left the millet seeds that he intended to plant at home, he despatched his son to get them. It was very hot and the son took a very long time on his errand. When he finally arrived he handed an iron pot to his father containing the seeds which he had cooked. Jock asked me to put myself in the place of the accused. He had waited in the heat for most of the morning and part of the afternoon for his seeds and when his son arrived he presented him with a dish of porridge. This splendid address was delivered in a broad Scottish accent and certainly influenced the court.

One afternoon Jock came to see me accompanied by the doctor, Don King, whom he said was to be his witness. I knew they had been away from the station for a few days on an investigation into an alleged murder. Jock told me his story.

The alleged murder was supposed to have taken place in the far north of the district deep in the bush and close to the border with the Caprivi Strip. A policeman knew where the body had been buried and Jock took the doctor along so that he could do a post mortem examination on the spot. If he found no evidence of foul play this would make it unnecessary to cart the decaying body back to Maun which was about 250 miles away.

The burial spot was in thick bush on very heavy sand about 20 odd miles west of the vehicle track which skirted the edge of the swamps so Jock decided to use horses to get to it. The black constables were well used to riding but neither the doctor nor Jock had ever ridden a horse and, not surprisingly, after 10 miles or so, they were very saddle sore. Although it was only late afternoon they decided to make camp. After an early supper the weary Jock, clad only in football shorts, went to sleep on the ground using his saddle as a pillow.

Later when it was dark he woke with a start and hearing the doctor who was lying nearby, cough, began describing the vivid dream which had awakened him. He said in the dream he felt that everything was pressing him down almost to suffocation point and he was very frightened. The doctor said that people who had experienced a severe disturbance to their sub-conscious state sometimes experienced such dreams. Jock, lying on his back with his arm behind his head on the saddle pillow, listened with interest. He then told the doctor that there seemed to be a heavy weight on his calves – he had his legs crossed at the ankles.

Don King switched on his torch and directed the beam at Jock's lower limbs but quickly switched it off and hissed at him not to move. Jock asked why and Don again hissed at him not to move adding that there was a big snake wrapped round his legs. Jock said he jerked involuntarily but otherwise lay still.

However, he must have disturbed the snake and it began to move up his right leg. He felt its head slither up his shorts but when it reached his crotch it must have realised it had come to a dead end because it withdrew and glided up through the thick hairs on his chest. When it reached the base of his neck it paused and raising its head peered first right and then left. Jock was lying with his head on one side and by looking down could see it quite clearly in the firelight. It then glided over his exposed neck and over the saddle. It would have disappeared into the night if one of the constables hadn't killed it with a thick stick he had picked up for this purpose whilst watching the snake's progress up Jock's body. Jock told me that when the snake was gliding over his neck it felt just like a baby's arm seeking comfort. But it was far from being as harmless as a baby's arm – it was a black mamba measuring over five feet.

Jock said he had brought the doctor to be his witness because he thought I would not believe his story. When later he repeated his story in Riley's bar the assembled company listened in total fascination. A curious effect of the encounter was that Jock gave up strong liquor for quite a while because he thought he owed his Maker something. The Maun crowd thought it odd that he should think the Maker was against strong drink. But Jock's sobriety did not last long and a year or so later he developed quite a serious drink problem. It cost him his wife and son but he pulled himself together, remarried and emigrated to Australia, started life anew and prospered.

The old man and the cigarette

My office in Maun was a rondavel – a round building with a thatched roof. From my office I had a slanting view of the river which was home to vast numbers of birds. The fish eagle was my favourite – its haunting cry seemed to come from the very soul of mysterious Africa.

Across a dusty space that sported a flagpole, were the square office blocks of the police and the agricultural and livestock officers. The modest courthouse was between them. The stark white of these buildings was relieved by a rectangle of grass with a round flowerbed in the middle. The paths were edged with whitewashed stones. My rondavel was circled by a narrow strip of grass and cannas grew against the wall.

These little gardens were tended by an old man. He was black and had tight, white, curly hair. He was a prisoner in the government gaol and his job was to water the grass and flowers with water drawn by the bucket from a tap near the courthouse. It was not a heavy job because he was an old man and I made sure his prison life was as comfortable as possible. This old man was in prison because of a tragic accident. This is what happened.

One Christmas morning I was sitting on the Residency lawn enjoying the cool shade of a huge flame tree which dominated my garden. Later on I was due to have Christmas dinner with my neighbour Captain Webb who was OC Police. I was a bachelor and Webby's wife had invited me out of kindness. They had a daughter just out of her teens and I suppose I was regarded as eligible.

I was watching the bird life on the river that flowed past the bottom of my garden when I sensed I was no longer alone. Turning my head slightly I saw an old man squatting respectfully to my right and just behind me. He raised his hand slightly when he saw that I had seen him and greeted me in the gentle, prolonged manner that is the African way and I returned his courtesies.

I knew the old man. He used to come to my office every month with a slip of paper for me to sign to certify that he was still alive. He was a pensioner having served as a policeman in one of the mine compounds in South Africa. He needed proof of his existence to draw his modest pension from the post office. He always impressed me with his dignity. He was the sort of person who could be totally respectful without the slightest trace of servility.

When the old man appeared on my front lawn I thought at first that he had come seeking a Christmas gift but I immediately dismissed this unworthy thought from my mind. After we had finished the greetings courtesies we sat quietly. I didn't feel in the least uncomfortable and was simply enjoying the peace that the old man seemed to have brought with him. It was as though he had come on a visit to an old friend.

However I became uneasy when, speaking softly and looking at the grass between his bare feet, he said he was in big trouble. When I asked him what sort of trouble, he said he had killed his wife earlier that morning and he had come to tell me about it.

Just at that moment my house-servant came out to see if I needed anything and, as he spoke good English, I asked him to stay and help. I indicated two chairs on the lawn but both of them, the old man and Sebogile, squatted in front of me. I noticed the respect with which Sebogile treated the old man. He greeted him humbly addressing him as "ntate" – an indication of respectful tenderness. The old man acknowledged this with a slight nod and proceeded to tell us about the big trouble.

He had, he said, daughters but no son and his wife had long passed childbearing age. He wanted a son and, after discussing matters with his wife, he took a much younger second wife. The young woman did not like this arrangement but had to obey her father and came to live in the old man's kraal when the bride price of cattle had been paid.

The young wife led the old man a merry dance and often sneaked off to enjoy the company of younger men. He remonstrated with her frequently but she took no notice. That morning she had returned to the old man's kraal after an all-night absence. He was sitting outside his hut on a heavy stool carved out of a solid piece of mahogany and shaped like an egg-timer.

The old man was very angry and shouted at the young woman about the disgrace she was bringing on him. She in turn swore at him and said "his balls were empty". Mad with rage, the old man jumped up, grabbed the stool by its narrow waist and threw it at the young woman who by then was retreating hastily. Just at that moment the senior wife came out of the hut where she had been sleeping and the heavy stool hit her behind the ear. She dropped down dead.

I was appalled. Sebogile and the old man sat with bowed heads and nothing was said for many moments. I remember well that whilst we were sitting in silence, the cry of the fish eagle came floating off the river. In my pity for the old man I somehow felt nearer to God then than at any other time in my life before or since.

However the law had to take its course and the old man was charged with murder. I presided over the preparatory examination even though I was aware of the facts of the case because all

I had to do was to record the evidence in writing and send the papers to the Attorney General for him to decide what action should be taken. He would decide whether to bring the case to the High Court or instruct the lower court to pass sentence with whatever increased jurisdiction was authorised by the Chief Justice.

So I sadly recorded the evidence. The old man spoke at length when he gave his evidence. When he came to the saddest part of his story he said how much he had loved his old wife, how good she had been to him, how they had lived in perfect harmony and how sad she had been that they had not produced a son. He said she had been very sick of late – sometimes so sick "that she could hardly carry the water from the river to the kraal". He was so concerned about her health that he used to walk the six miles to the mission hospital to get pills for her!

Describing the stool throwing, he said he really meant to kill his young wife. I gently interrupted him because, I didn't want him to incriminate himself unnecessarily. I tried, perhaps not very judicially and rather obliquely, to get him to leave this bit about intent out.

When this was interpreted to him, he listened gravely, thought for a moment and then spoke softly. When he had finished the interpreter stood in silence, shuffling his feet in a rather embarrassed manner. I asked him what the old man had said. Not looking me in the eye, the interpreter said that the old man had said that I had asked him to take an oath on the Bible to speak the truth and the truth was that he had meant to kill his young wife and now I didn't want him to tell the truth. I bowed my head in shame and the old man went on to finish his statement.

The papers were sent off and after a few weeks came back with my jurisdiction increased to four years which, with a very heavy heart, was the sentence I imposed. And that is how the old man came to spend his days watering the gardens around the government offices.

He had to walk over to the little garden around my office with his bucket that he filled from the tap near the courthouse. One day, after I finished hearing a case, I left a folder on the bench in the courtroom. As the old man had to return to the tap for water, I asked him to pick up the folder and bring it to my office.

He returned almost proudly with it and, leaving his prison hat on the doorstep, padded into my office in his bare feet. He handed me the folder in that wonderfully courteous African manner with the fingers of the right hand touching his arm just above the wrist of the hand holding the folder. I gave him two cigarettes from the packet on my desk and he regarded me with a surprised look. I told him to go behind my office and take a break. He looked at me like a fond father regarding a naughty but favourite child, murmured his thanks and padded out.

A few days later I was hearing a bundle of petty court cases. Having dealt with one, I was writing something in the records and, on looking up, I was startled to see the old man in the dock. I looked at the charge sheet – an offence against the prison regulations – being found in possession of tobacco. The exhibit, which was placed before me, was one half-smoked cigarette.

I read out the charge and asked the old man how he pleaded. He smiled at me with everything but his mouth and then humbly pleaded guilty. I said I would put him on probation and pass sentence on a certain date that was a few months after his release – years hence.

Webby, who had been prosecuting, came over to my cool rondavel later that morning to check on my sanity I suppose but after I had confessed to my part in the crime he agreed that justice had been done.

Webby

Captain Charles Adam Webb was OC Police in Maun for part of my time there. He was a great Bechuanaland character, known as Webby to everyone except his wife who called him Adam. He was quite short. He was bald and he strutted. He reminded me of Toad. But he was a good, fair and courageous policemen and despite being a stern disciplinarian was very kind to those under his command albeit in a paternalistic sort of way.

He was very fond of me and used to fuss about me as though I were his son. He was usually whistling rather tunelessly whilst he bustled about his business and popped in to my office frequently for tea or a chat during which he often came out with some scurrilous piece of information – for instance a rather haughty lady on the station had "a touch of the tar brush, old chap", how I should never trust an African who wore sunglasses and sported a beard – Communists old chap!

Another piece of misinformation he passed on to me was that a District Officer called Batho was really called Botha. He had changed it because when he applied for a post in the administration he knew that an Afrikaner would never be accepted. In fact the name Batho is of Cornish origin and there was absolutely no evidence that he had ever changed his name.

He seemed to be proud that I was a Cambridge man and was a District Officer. When I collected my MA he was most impressed. When I told him it was more or less automatic I think he wished I hadn't. We often went on tour together and in our leisure moments he would keep me entertained with an endless flow of chatter. Sometimes he would nod off almost in mid sentence and when he awoke with a start he would simply carry on from where he had left off and this would happen even if the nodding off was followed by a night's sleep! He was, I'm afraid, a bit of a Munchausen but his stories harmed nobody and I think he told them to puff out his self-importance. But some of his tales were true and I enjoyed trying to separate the believable from the rest.

I didn't believe for instance that he once played rugby for the Racing Club of France and that in the dying moments of a hard fought game responded to the exhortation of the French specta- tors to 'droppa la keek' by scoring the winning points. Nor did I believe that he was once best man at the wedding of a Hungarian princess and wore a purple double-breasted suit at the ceremony that took place in the cathedral in Vienna. I also thought it most unlikely that whilst kneeling beside her at the altar rail (a part of the functions of the best man which remained unexplained) that she whispered in his ear that he was a "handsome brute".

But there were other stories about him that were confirmed by reliable sources. Once in the 1930s he was out riding for pleasure with a stock inspector called George Watson. Webby paused beside a tall anthill and picked a fungus that was growing on its sloping side. George warned him that it was poisonous but Webby replied scornfully that his wife often served them at home and popped it in his mouth. George replied that they were fine cooked but poisonous raw but Webby had already swallowed it. A short while later he complained of stomach cramps and after a while slithered off his horse. George slung him across the saddle with difficulty because, even when he was younger Webby was quite rotund, and eventually got him to the mission hospital where he told the young doctor what had happened. They got him onto a bed and the doctor went to work. After prodding and peering he announced that he was afraid the stricken Webby "had gone" at which the 'corpse' croaked "Have I hell". The riding companion's advice was "Shut up Webby – the doctor knows what he is doing."

On another occasion when he was a young trooper he was ordered to report to police headquarters for some official purpose. Whilst searching for the office of the person he had to report to he was accosted by the camp commandant who was on horseback leading a mounted troop. The camp commandant was a short tempered, fiery little man and he barked at the young trooper that he was rehearsing for a police parade and wanted to ensure that the horses would not shy away from the spectators when they applauded the appearance of the troop. He told Webby to leap out waving his arms when he rounded a nearby building leading his troop.

Webby did as he as told but the horses ignored him and the commandant cursed him for putting on a feeble show. They tried again with the same result. The furious commandant swore at Webby and said he had better put on a more realistic act for the third attempt or he would crucify him.

Whilst Webby was positioning himself, a prison working party came round the corner so he got the convicts to huddle against the building with him and told them that when the horses appeared they must leap out shouting and waving their picks and shovels. This they did and the effect was spectacular. The horses bolted. Webby decided to hop it but the commandant having got his terrified horse under control spotted him sprinting towards the office block and drawing his ceremonial sword galloped after him. Webby got himself down a narrow alleyway between two offices so the enraged and mounted commandant couldn't reach him with his sword thrusts and snorting prodigiously, he eventually cantered off to round up his scattered troop. Webby told me he was sure that if the commandant had managed to get him within range he would have stuck him like a pig.

Most people who were stationed at the remote desert station of Tshabong were captivated by the beautiful loneliness of the place. Webby was no exception and often spoke about his time there. He was pleased that I had been stationed there. He told me that once when he was in charge of the station because the District Commissioner was on leave, a Bushman band came to the office and reported that they had heard a very loud bang deep in the desert. Webby composed a radio message reporting the incident to send to headquarters but on his way to the radio room had second thoughts and decided not to send it because the people in Mafikeng might have thought he had been in the desert too long.

The District Commissioner at that time was a rather eccentric ex-army man – he liked to be referred to as major. He was also a very competent Persian linguist and had a good translation of the Rubaiyat to his credit. His other main interest in life was an undying hatred of poachers especially if they were Afrikaners from across the border of his desert domain. I think he was more interested in the welfare of the desert wildlife than in that of the human inhabitants of his district.

Webby told me he was once out on patrol with the major when they came across a poaching party with a number of springbok loaded on the back of a three ton truck. The poachers set off for the border and safety, driving recklessly across country with Webby in hot pursuit. When they got within range the major drew his revolver, instructed Webby to "press home the attack Inspector and maintain speed" and, after a couple of attempts, shot off one of the rear tyres of the truck.

Webbie also recounted how the same major, determined to do things in style for a visit to Tshabong by the High Commissioner, tried to organise a spectacular welcome for the visiting dignitaries. He fitted the back of his open pick-up truck with seats because he planned to drive the visiting party from the landing strip to his house escorted by the police camel patrol flying their pennants. He had also arranged for about 50 villagers to be at the landing strip with their horses so they could bring up the rear in durbar fashion.

The plane landed and the major got the High Commissioner, his lady and the Private Secretary seated. The villagers had respectfully dismounted when the ostrich feather-plumed High Commissioner climbed out of the aircraft and despite much arm waving by the major from his driving seat they were reluctant to remount. Furious, he leapt out and striding across the landing strip brandishing his pith helmet, whilst well within earshot of the High Commissioner and his lady who with fixed smiles were waving gracefully to the sullen crowd, bawled at the villagers "Mount you stupid bastards – mount".

An outbreak of rabies

Soon after I recovered from the malaria I contracted on the Chanoga fishing trip I had to seek medical attention again. I had a magnificent black bull terrier dog called Butch. Webby had a white bitch called Susie. We mated them and a litter of six was the result. Shortly before the pups were born I woke up one morning to find Butch stiff and cold at the foot of my bed. He had died during the night. He had been out of sorts for a while. I realised he wasn't well because he wouldn't come to the office with me or accompany me if I went to Rileys in the evening but the vet could not diagnose what was wrong with him.

I claimed a pup from Susie's litter as Butch's stud fee and chose a lovely white male. I christened him Abdul. Another pup went to the Agricultural Officer and the others to various people on the station. One morning when the Agricultural Officer's handyman was mowing the lawn, his pup tried to bite the revolving blades of the hand-propelled mower. When the handyman stopped and pushed the puppy away it bit him on the ankle. Webby's wife Molly was also bitten by a pup they had kept when she stopped it worrying a mat in the kitchen. These incidents were largely ignored at the time and their dreadful significance emerged only later.

Shortly after these happenings I was reading on my stoep one evening and I noticed that Abdul was very restless. He kept starting up and running about but when I comforted him he quietened down after much wriggling and hand licking. When I went to bed I wrapped him in a blanket and took him with me. He was soon asleep and I followed him only to be woken shortly after by his licking my face and chest in a very excited state. I gathered him up and put him in an empty servant's quarter outside and went back to bed.

Before sunrise the next morning my house servant woke me and said the police radio operator wanted to speak to me urgently. When I went out the operator handed me a radio message. It was from the Agricultural Officer who had left on tour a few days before, taking with him his servant who had been bitten – the Agricultural Officer had witnessed this incident. The message was to say that the servant was in Livingstone hospital dying from the incurable disease of hydrophobia.

I guessed immediately what was wrong with Abdul and took my .22 rifle and shot him through the open window of the servant's quarter. I then alerted the police commander and the vet who dealt with the remaining puppies. An aeroplane happened to be on the station and was bound for Johannesburg that morning so the vet packed the puppies' brains in specimen jars and despatched them to the South African Institute of Medical Research. We received a telegraphed reply the next morning confirming that the brains were all from dogs positive for rabies.

When I was having lunch I received a message from the doctor asking me to go and see him so off I went. He asked me about Abdul and I told him what had happened. He said I had better have the rabies inoculations. I protested that Abdul had not bitten me but he pointed out that one's hands often have small cuts and a man who shaved usually had small nicks on his face. So I had my first painful injection in the stomach – the site chosen because 13 more had to follow and after the first four finding a relatively untender place was more or less possible over a large area of flesh.

After the injection we repaired to the doctor's house next to the hospital to have a cup of tea and whilst waiting for it to be brewed I took a medical textbook from the bookcase and looked up the section dealing with rabies. I noticed the warning that a fairly high percentage of those undergoing inoculation treatment suffered a 'neuro-paralytic accident'. When the doctor brought in the tea I asked what this meant in layman's terms. He replied rather cheerfully that it meant more or less that the patient dropped dead.

Patients receiving the inoculations were advised not to drink alcohol but that evening I was feeling a bit low. The 'neuro-paralytic accident' business made me feel uneasy more particularly because I was experiencing the side effects of the inoculation – a throbbing headache and girdle pains. I thought what the hell and decided that a few beers in cheerful company at Rileys would lift my flagging spirits. When I entered the bar I found the company was far from cheerful. Most of the drinkers were also being jabbed in the stomach. When Chobo Weskob walked in with his Jack Russell at his heels the drinkers on the stools raised their feet to the next rung and those in chairs tucked their feet under them. Those standing made space between them and the harmless fox terrier. When I remarked on this we all had a bit of a laugh. But tragedy was to strike a week or so later.

The doctor called at my house one evening and said he had just come from the Webbs and was very worried about Molly who was seriously ill. He told me that after she had been bitten she refused to have the injections because she had had a very adverse reaction in the past from a penicillin injection. She was a trained nurse and I thought her refusal to start the course of inoculations for this reason astonishing. So did the doctor but, as he said, he couldn't force her to undergo treatment but he had kept at her and after ten days or so she agreed. But by then it was too late.

The next morning we flew her out to Bulawayo for specialist attention. I went to see her off at the landing strip and made some cheerful remark about how she would soon be back with us. She just looked at me and shook her head and I knew that she knew. She died a few days later.

It was a bad time on the station. These two avoidable deaths within the space of a few weeks in the close-knit community had a very bad effect on morale. Webby and his children – two sons and a daughter – were devastated. Molly had been the lynch pin of the family and had been taken from them at such short notice. Oddly enough Susie, the bull terrier bitch, was not infected and in a curious way seemed to be of great comfort to Webby. However, the Government acted quickly and moved him to a line station to get him away from some of his sadness. But he was a sturdy fellow and it was not too long before he was back to his normal self – at least outwardly but I knew him well and know that he never really got over Molly's death.

Top: crossing the flooded Shashi river.

Below: the causeway at Samadupi near Maun after floods.
Photographs by Noel Redman.

Top: cattle crossing the Zambezi at Kazangula. Photograph by Noel Redman.

Below: Ted Warren (BP Police) on left with Lionel Palmer, then an Agricultural Officer, on trek with donkeys in tsetse country in Ngamiland in 1952. Photograph supplied by Lionel Palmer.

Top: the Maun caboose team. From left, unknown passenger, Thomas Allifeyo, Montsho Mogolakwe (sub-chief at Sehitwa), Jack Ramsden, Kambo Kambo, 'Poons' Mapunya.

Below: The caboose stuck in 'black turf' in Ngamiland in 1957. Photographs by MRB Williams.

Top: Regent of the Batawana, Mrs Moremi, opening a school in 1958. Photograph by MRB Williams.

Below: Herero woman and baby.

Top: Herero gathering in 1958. Photograph by MRB WIlliams.

Below: the Queen's birthday parade in Maun in 1958 with the District Commissioner MRB Williams inspecting Girl Guides. Photograph supplied by MRB Williams.

Top: Captain AC Webb (Webby) making friends with a group of Bushman women in the Kalahari. Photograph by MRB Williams.

Above: Colonel Bob Langley with a mounted police escort. Photograph by Noel Redman.

CHAPTER 6

SOUTH TO LOBATSE

Shortly after the outbreak of rabies I received a posting order from headquarters informing me that I was to take over as District Commissioner in Lobatse that was on the line of rail in the south about 30 miles north of Mafikeng. I wasn't very pleased because Lobatse was far too 'civilised' for my taste and I knew I would miss the carefree life of the north-west.

I was given a splendid send-off party that was also attended by the person I was handing over to – a District Officer called Eustace Clark. Eustace was a pleasant chap and being an old Etonian was much more conscious of his dignity than I was. I thought the Maun crowd would soon tame him. He had his first taste of their rather relaxed attitude to life at my farewell party. Jock Allan had composed a farewell song for me which went to the tune of Uncle Tom Cobbley. All I can remember is the chorus that went "Jan Vermaak, Eustace Clark, Ivor Lewis of the tsetse, Ruth and Seretse, Old Uncle Tom Kays and all, Old Uncle Tom Kays and all." I could tell by the expression on Eustace's face when the chorus was bawled out that he did not like being coupled with Jan Vermaak who was a Public Works Department road foreman.

The next day I said my last farewells and set off for Lobatse. It was a long journey so I spent the night in Francistown before making my way south to my new station. I was taking over from my old friend Norman Matthews. He was standing in for the Divisional Commissioner who was on long leave and I was looking forward to working with him again.

I had been invited to stay with the station doctor's family in Lobatse before moving into the rambling residency. I was told later that the doctor's wife particularly wanted me to stay because she did not approve of her daughter's fiancé and thought I might cause her to switch her affections. However, it didn't work that way – the daughter and I were good friends but no more than that. The doctor's wife was correct in her disapproval of the prospective son-in-law because he later spent time in prison for fraud and eventually committed suicide.

Norman Matthews was a changed man. He had stopped drinking and his wife was greatly relieved. She told me it was so nice to be able to buy bits and pieces to make her house pretty again. It was good to be working with Norman once more. He and his wife had moved out of the residency into the Divisional Commissioner's house and had left most of their personal furniture for my use so I was very comfortable – more so than in my up-to-now rather sparsely furnished bachelor quarters.

Lobatse was a rather rural station but I enjoyed my time there. Most of the district outside the township was state land settled by white farmers but part of it was occupied by the Barolong tribe that straddled the border, most of them living in the Mafikeng area. They were very advanced agriculturally and I remember one man in particular who was an outstanding farmer. He started life with very little and was employed for some years in some lowly capacity in some shop in Mafikeng. He was a yard labourer or something like that because in those days black men were not allowed to serve white people in European shops! He saved up and bought a plough that he dismantled and took over the border in convenient loads on his bicycle to where he had been allocated a patch of land by the chief. He sold his wife's sewing machine and bought a mule and started farming. When I knew him he had become prosperous and owned a tractor and trailer.

He had been granted master farmer status by the Agricultural Department and on one occasion his farm was chosen as the site for a farmers' day ceremony organised by the Agricultural Officer. He was questioned closely by the other farmers about when he had ploughed, what seeds he had used and many other questions about why his crops were in such good condition. He answered all the questions fluently and fully after consulting a little black notebook that he was carrying. My interpreter was standing next to him interpreting for my benefit and he told me later that the farmer was holding the notebook up side down – his wife was the literate member of the family but the husband had a good memory.

The High Court

The High Court was situated in Lobatse. The jury system was not used in Bechuanaland possibly because of the difficulty of selecting twelve members of the public who were without serious bias. Instead the judge sat with assessors – two black and two white – who advised him but the final verdict of guilty or not lay with the presiding officer. The white assessors were usually District Officers who had magisterial experience and the black assessors were tribal elders well versed in customary law. Because I was on hand in Lobatse I was frequently called upon to act as an assessor.

One case on which I was an assessor involved a South African police constable called Kroucamp. The allegation was that he had pursued a black burglar from the village of Alldays in the Transvaal across the border into Bechuanaland where he had shot and killed him. He had transported the body back to

Alldays and had buried the corpse in the grounds of the police station there. I think that this is exactly what had happened but he had a very good defence lawyer who managed to convince the judge that the police constable had acted in self-defence at the scene of the killing.

The judge was Irish and very long winded. He took ages over his summing up. The accused was a runtish little man who had lost a lot of weight during his week-long trial. The judge droned on and it was not at all clear which way the verdict would go. Murder was punishable by hanging so the accused was understandingly concerned at what the verdict would be.

Because the judge was taking an inordinate length of time in his summing up the court usher had miscalculated the time that the next case would begin and he had gathered the numerous witnesses involved on the verandah outside the court. The crowd was growing restive and the chatter increased in volume. The judge interrupted his tedious summing up and instructed the court usher to silence those people who were "hanging" about outside the court. At the mention of the dread word the accused paled and winced.

On another occasion when Sir Walter Harrigan was presiding over a case the defence attorney took a very long time in declaiming why his client should be found not guilty. It was a very hot day and the rather testy judge was suffering in his heavy robes. He was also convinced that the accused was guilty so he found the defence attorney's drone particularly tedious. He leant forward over the bench to address the Registrar who was seated at a table in the well of the court and hissed "What is this bloody man's name?" The Registrar hissed over his shoulder "Language, my Lord". Harrigan shot back "Never mind my bloody language, what is the man's name?" The Registrar replied "His name is Language my Lord".

Shortly after the second world war there was a long trial in the High Court involving rice which was being smuggled out of Southern Rhodesia through Bechuanaland and into South Africa where it was expensive and in short supply. Half way through the case the judge, who was staying in the only hotel in Lobatse was attending to his morning needs in the communal toilet block and from behind his locked door heard two of the defence witnesses, who were washing and shaving in the row of wash basins, discussing what the defence attorney had instructed them to say in the witness box, all of which was balderdash as they jokingly admitted to one another. The judge had to recuse himself and a new trial was arranged.

But before this interruption a man called Judge was summoned as a witness because at the time of the alleged offence he had been a checker at the Lobatse railway station. After he had given evidence the judge told him he was free to go but he said there was something he would like to say to the court. The surprised judge asked him what it was he wanted to say and the witness replied that when he had attempted to book in at the hotel he was told that there was no room. The judge said that this was nothing to do with the court and the witness said oh yes it had because the proprietor had said "We have one bloody judge too many in Lobatse at the moment". The outraged judge threw a cadenza but when he had calmed down he saw the funny side and told the witness to step down.

Graveside tales

Piet Odendaal was a driller at one time but when I met him first he had retired and lived in Lobatse. He had became a sort of odd job man and lived in a caravan. He was called upon from time to time to supervise road gangs and that sort of thing. Once when I was having a drink at the hotel Piet was drinking in the bar. He looked like a patriach and had a long grey beard. Sid Milner – the hotel owner – and I were chatting at the opposite end of the bar from where Piet was sitting and Sid told me how a couple of years earlier Piet had been far out in the Kalahari beyond one of the disease control fences drilling for water when his truck broke down. One of his labourers set off to walk back along the fence to get help. Sid, who was going on a hunting expedition, met him along the way and was told that Piet had been marooned for about a week. When Sid reached his camp Piet was sitting under a thorn tree in its shade and without getting up he asked Sid if he had any "dop" (Cape brandy). Sid handed over a bottle and Piet took a long satisfying swig. He wiped his hairy lips with the back of his hand and asked Sid if he had anything to eat.

In the mid sixties there was a foot and mouth outbreak and the cordon fences were manned and patrolled. Piet was taken on as a temporary foreman in charge of one of these gangs and set up his camp far out along the fence in the desert in the Serowe district. He was visited from time to time by a veterinary officer recently out from England. On one of the visits the vet discovered poor old Piet in his tent – he had died some days previously. His labourers thought he was just having a drink so they didn't disturb him but when he hadn't appeared for some time one of them peeped in and saw his body slumped in a chair. There was not much the labourers could do because although Piet had been issued with a government truck none of them could drive.

The young vet turned tail and went to report to the vet in charge of the district who when the report was made asked where Piet was and was told he was still in his tent. So the young vet was sent back with a policeman to bring him in. It was high summer so the task was rather gruesome. The senior vet told me that when they got Piet back to the station they decided to bury him as soon as the doctor had completed the post mortem examination. Apparently they had some difficulty squeezing Piet into the coffin but they managed – just. But when the coffin was off loaded and was being carried to the grave there was a snapping noise and the lid popped open down one side. Piet's arm shot out. The senior vet told me it was as though he was waving goodbye to the world.

There was another character on the station who was also a prodigious drinker. He was also a prodigious liar but everyone knew this and accepted him. He was called Upton – Uppie – and was a Rodent Inspector. His job was to control rodent outbreaks in villages because rats and mice created havoc with stored grain. He had been based in Maun because plagues of rats and mice had been reported in various parts of the district and the government feared an outbreak of bubonic plague such as that of the late 1930s. I think Uppie spent more time chasing the contents of bottles of cane spirit than he did chasing rats and mice.

I was stationed in Maun when he was there and he became quite friendly with the matron who was a middle-aged spinster. She didn't like me very much because I used to pull her leg and she didn't have much sense of humour. When I asked her when we would be hearing wedding bells she told me that unlike some people in Maun Mr Upton was a gentleman and his grandfather had been a cardinal!

Someone told me that later when he was based in Serowe a woman doctor was posted to the station and her house was next to his. She had a large, unusually coloured cat but shortly after she arrived on the station it disappeared. After about three weeks during which time she had not set eyes on her neighbour she decided to pay him a visit having ascertained from his servant that the master was there. Getting no reply to her knocking she cautiously pushed opened the verandah door and then moved across to the sitting room door that was ajar. The room was in semi-darkness because the skimpy curtains were drawn and when her eyes became accustomed to the gloom she saw Uppie dozing in an armchair. But the next thing she saw was her cat sitting on a low coffee table. She joyfully rushed across to pick it up but it was dead and stuffed. Later enquiries revealed that he had seen it in the bushes at the bottom of his garden and had thought it was a curious wild animal so he added it to his collection.

But eventually poor old Uppie succumbed to a bottle of vodka a day when he wasn't really trying and Norman Towell the OC Police in Lobatse had to arrange the funeral. He managed to rustle up a Roman Catholic priest to officiate and inspanned his sub inspectors to give Uppie a decent send off. One of them – Jud Brookes – was the most accident-prone man I have ever known. It was raining when they got to the open grave with the coffin and after they had put it down prior to the burial proper Jud started shuffling his feet. Norman hissed at him to stand still but Jud didn't seemed to understand what 'motionless' meant and carried on shuffling his huge feet. Norman told me he could see exactly what was about to happen and with a loud "Damn and blast" Jud fell into the grave and had to be hauled out.

On another occasion Jud was travelling north by train after a spell of leave and was in bed in the early morning when he woke up with a start thinking he had arrived at his destination. He stuck his huge head out of the window which was closed and gashed his forehead rather badly. He was hauled off the train so his wound could be attended to and by the time the doctor had finished stitching him up the train had departed. Jud got on the police radio to explain to the OC of the station up the line why his arrival would be delayed. When describing the window incident to his invisible audience he stuck out his arm to indicate what he did with his head and put his fist through the window of the radio room. He required several stitches in his arm. The OC Police is alleged to have said "Get this bastard back on the train before he wrecks the whole station."

Somebody told me that when Jud was on police duty with dogs in the UK he had to attend to a disorderly crowd and his own police dog "bit him in the backside".

A visit from Oliver Tambo

Little did I know when I was transferred to Lobatse that my bachelor days were drawing to a close and just before Christmas 1959 I met the woman who was to be my future wife. She was spending the Christmas holidays with her brother and his family. He was a geologist in the Department of Geological Survey and was based in Lobatse. After a brief courtship we decided to become engaged. Norman Matthews was absolutely delighted when I told him and made many telephone calls to people he thought should hear the good news. He organised an engagement dinner for us at his house. I remember his opening a bottle of his best wine and making the round of the table. When he came to his place he raised the bottle to his nose and breathed in lovingly and longingly. I glanced at his wife who was sitting up very straight at the bottom of the table with her eyes half closed and her lips moving very slightly. She relaxed when Norman put the bottle on the sideboard and filled his glass with Coca Cola.

My fiancée returned to Port Elizabeth in South Africa to serve out her notice in the library service and to prepare for our wedding in May. I stayed on in Lobatse because there didn't seem much for me to do except turn up at the church on the appointed day looking reasonably tidy.

However I soon had more than enough to do because at

about 4 am on Tuesday 22 March I was roused by a loud knocking on my door. It was Oliver Tambo the Secretary of the African National Congress who had come seeking political asylum in Bechuanaland. He told me that in the afternoon of the previous day the South African Police had shot and killed 60 Africans, mainly women, who were protesting about the pass laws in that country at a place called Sharpeville. A warrant had been issued for his arrest and he decided to flee the country. He was accompanied by a young white man called Ronald Segal. Oliver Tambo was very calm and in total control of whatever emotions were surging through him. His companion was however in a highly excited state. The adrenalin seemed to be surging through him and he kept gabbling on about "kragdadigheit". I didn't know what this meant but I gathered it meant something rather nasty and violent.

When Oliver left us to freshen himself up in the bathroom I asked young Segal what he thought was going to happen. He said that things had gone over the edge and there was going to be a bloodbath and the whites would get what was coming to them. I said I found this particularly disturbing because my fiancée was in Port Elizabeth. He told me to contact her as soon as possible and tell her to get out of the country.

When Oliver returned Segal left us alone whilst he used the bathroom and I told him about the advice to get my fiancée out of South Africa. He just smiled and said Segal was over-excited and there was not going to be a blood bath.

Segal decided to return to South Africa and he left Oliver Tambo and me to sit out what remained of the night. There was little I could do because the telephones did not become operational until 8 a.m. or so and I needed some advice from headquarters as I was a bit out of my depth when it came to requests for political asylum. We chatted over numerous cups of tea and I was totally impressed by Tambo. He told me that ever since its formation in 1912 the African National Congress had tried to come to a reasonable and peaceful accommodation with the whites but every approach had been rebuffed and indignity after indignity had been heaped on the black people. He said he was determined not to give up but when he had been tipped off about the warrant for his arrest he had come to the conclusion that he would not be able to do much from a prison cell which was why he had taken the desperate decision to flee. I got the impression that he had fled the country not because he was afraid of the South African Police but because he was determined to secure justice for the blacks in his country. He believed he could do this by persuasion and by bringing international pressures to bear on the Nationalist Government.

He was afraid of being returned to South Africa by the Bechuanaland government and I told him I thought this was most unlikely. He was also afraid of being kidnapped by the South African Police and I said I thought this also was unlikely because of the international row that would follow such an outrage.

I contacted Arthur Douglas the Administrative Secretary at the headquarters in Mafikeng by telephone as soon as I could and he told me I had better find some safe accommodation for Oliver Tambo and come down to see him so we could decide on a way forward. He was a fine man. He was Scottish and completely unflappable. Some thought him pompous but he wasn't – I think he adopted this pose to cover up his shyness. He was a very able administrator and I was relieved to hand over the problem to him. I made sure Oliver Tambo was suitably housed and went down to Mafikeng. The upshot was that political asylum was granted and Oliver Tambo soon departed for Zambia on his way farther north – well out of the clutches of the South African Police.

Wedding bells

I was pleased I hadn't urged Bridget to make a panic stricken flight from South Africa and she arrived in Lobatse as planned about three weeks before the date fixed for the wedding. This was to take place in the delightful little stone church in the village and the reception was to be held in the garden of Chris and Jeanne Jennings' (my future brother and sister in-laws) house. Once I had supplied the list of my guests there didn't seem much for me to do. Norman Matthews had taken over from me as District Commissioner and there wasn't much for me to do in the office.

However Norman soon found something for me to do. He received a radio message from the OC Police at Tshabong saying that someone was needed to try a court case at Bokspits, a village in the extreme south west corner of Bechuanaland deep in the Kalahari. Norman asked if I would go and I leapt at the chance to revisit my old district. The OC Police – Frank Woods – was running the show at the time because the District Commissioner was on leave but naturally he did not have magisterial powers. I asked Norman if I could take Bridget with me and as we would be chaperoned by Frank Woods (and his wife) permission was granted!

We spent a weekend in Tshabong and then accompanied by Dinah and Frank Woods made the long trip down the Molopo to Bokspits. When we got there we discovered it would not be possible to hold court because an essential witness had failed to turn up. We decided to camp for the night at the entrance to the Gemsbok National Park before trekking back to Tshabong.

First we called on Klaas van der Westhuizen who was a good friend of mine. He was the local storekeeper and the unofficial mayor of the community. He was a remarkable man. He couldn't have had much formal education but he was well endowed with wisdom and good judgement. He had made a great contribution to the prosperity of the villagers by persuading them by example to take up karakul sheep farming. He was very pleased to see me and insisted on having one of his biggest cockerels slaughtered and he presented it to me for my evening meal.

When we established camp Bridget offered to cook the bird. She decided it would be best to make a chicken stew and managed to get the rather large bird into a pot. She cooked it for a long time but she had no experience of cooking an aged Kalahari cockerel and the result was very chewy.

After supper we were sitting at the camp table by the light of the moon, stars and campfire when she decided perhaps to apologise for the tough fowl or show some affection for me by massaging my foot with hers under the table. After fishing around she found what she thought was my foot but was surprised that she got no reaction from me but she persisted. She noticed after a few moments that the police escort was looking very uncomfortable and when she glanced under the table she saw my feet were tucked under my chair and her foot was hooked around Frank Woods'! In her embarrassment nothing was said so Frank probably had some strange ideas about how long the impending marriage would last.

When we returned to Lobatse there was a posting order waiting for me informing me that on my return to duty in June I would be stationed in Mochudi as District Commissioner of the Bakgatla tribe. So I had a honeymoon to look forward to and a good posting on my return. Life was very sweet indeed.

At this time Webby was stationed on the line of rail in Mahalapye – the station to which he had been posted after the death in Maun of his wife Molly. Naturally he received an invitation to the wedding and immediately sent me a radio message saying that I couldn't possible take my wife on honeymoon in a one and a half ton Bedford truck which was my chosen form of transport in those days and he offered to lend me his smart Chevrolet Imp saloon. This was typical of the kind fellow. I think he regarded Bridget as his future daughter-in-law!

The day of the wedding soon arrived and a large contingent of my colleagues and friends attended. Webby of course was amongst them and he arrived very early and sought out Dave Robinson – my best man – and me – we were staying with the Matthews. He was anxious to meet the future bride and we told him she was to be found at her brother's house. He knew Chris Jennings and he also knew that he had played rugby for Natal University and for the Province and this made him something special.

So the chattering Webby bustled up to see Bridget who was on the point of leaving for a hair appointment. Webby accompanied her and kept up his endless flow of chatter even when she was under the hair drier – he simply got closer and shouted. Inspired by her brother's rugby history no doubt he even managed to get in his story about how he scored the winning drop kick when he played for the Racing Club of France. This was Bridget's first meeting with Webby and I suppose she must have thought some of my friends were very odd indeed.

After a wonderful wedding in the gorgeous early winter sunshine and a memorable month visiting Bridget's old haunts in South Africa we returned to Bechuanaland with a pleasant bump and made our way to Mochudi.

Above: the High Court
building in Lobatse.
Photograph by
Noel Redman.

Above and right:
GW and Bridget on
their wedding day in
Lobatse, May 1960.
Photographs by
Irene Jennings.

CHAPTER 7

THE BAKGATLA

Mochudi is the capital of the Bakgatla Tribal Territory – the Kgatleng – situated in the south-eastern part of Bechuanaland. The territory is quite hilly and enjoys relatively high rainfall. The valleys offer favourable areas for cultivation. When I was stationed there in the early 1960s the total population of the district was probably about 50,000 but as there had never been an accurate census nobody could tell for sure. A large proportion of the total population lived in Mochudi. The Residency that was to be our future home was attractively sited on a small kopje called Phapane about a mile from the outskirts of the village.

The Bakgatla are an interesting people. They originated in the Transvaal and in the early 19th century suffered severely from the depredations of Msilikazi's raiding parties. Later the Boers in the Transvaal claimed the right to tax the tribesmen – a claim that was fiercely resisted. The climax came when Paul Kruger publicly flogged the Bakgatla Chief Kgamanyane for failing to provide native labour to work on the Boer farms. The Bakwena invited the chief to bring his people to live in Bechuanaland and so in 1871 he established the tribal headquarters at Mochudi. The Bakwena claimed the Bakgatla as their subjects as did the Transvaal Boers but the Bakgatla resisted these claims fiercely and aggressively. Eventually in 1899 the Bechuanaland Protectorate Administration confirmed the right of the Bakgatla to the territory they were occupying and fixed the boundaries.

From 1920 to 1929 Isang was the regent because the heir

to the chieftainship (Molefi) was a minor. Isang was very progressive and established a large school with a European principal in Mochudi. This was built with funds provided by a special levy on tribesmen who were required to work in the Transvaal gold mines to provide the money. He was also very active in agricultural matters. He established a bull camp and introduced a syndicate system of borehole development and ownership. In 1929 Molefi came of age and Isang ceased to take an active part in tribal affairs. He died in 1946.

Molefi assumed the chieftainship but proved to be very impetuous and unbalanced in his behaviour. The main problem was that he drank too much and in 1935 he was suspended from office and his brother Mmusi became acting chief. Molefi continued to behave badly and in 1937 he was banished from the tribal territory. He was very quick to join up and in the Second World War became a Regimental Sergeant Major in the pioneer corps raised in Bechuanaland. He was at home in the army and loved to wear his uniform on special occasions long after he returned to civilian life.

I first met Molefi in 1956 when I was on tour in the Tuli Block. He and a large crowd of his followers were on their way to visit his mother who lived on a farm called Lentswe la Moriti near the junction of the Macloutsie and the Limpopo rivers. The reason why his mother lived there was that he had banished her and her attendants from the tribal territory because they belonged to the Zionist African Church and he regarded this church as subversive to his authority. The Zionist Church bought the farm so Molefi's mother and her companions had somewhere to live. When I met him he was dressed in his Regimental Sergeant Major's uniform urging his followers to dig out the bus in which they were travelling that was bogged down in the heavy sand of the dry Macloutsie river bed.

Despite his problematic behaviour and his heavy drinking he was a most engaging man. Some of his exploits were legendary. The Dutch Reformed Church had a mission station in Mochudi and had built a large church there. Molefi was frequently at odds with the dominie in charge of the mission and once during one of these disputes he rode his white horse up the steps of the church and down the aisle and drove the congregation out with his whip. On another occasion he was in Mafikeng when his truck developed some engine trouble. He stopped at one of the garages, strode into the workshop and on seeing a pair of legs protruding from under a vehicle, grabbed hold of the mechanic by the ankles, hauled him out and told him to fix his truck. The mechanic was a burly Afrikaner with very traditional views about 'kaffirs'. A fierce fistfight ensued. Molefi was a big man but was no match for the enraged mechanic who eventually floored his opponent. Molefi picked himself up, retrieved his hat, shook the mechanic's hand and asked him to fix up his truck and he did!

However, I never had the pleasure or frustration of working with Molefi because a few months before I was posted to Mochudi he turned his truck over on the road just outside the residency and was killed. He had been drinking at the time. His son and heir was a minor so once again his brother Mmusi became the acting chief and the young boy was sent to England to complete his education.

Soon after I arrived in Mochudi I called upon Mmusi by appointment to introduce myself. He had the royal headmen with him and I must say I found them an impressive lot – they must have been to have put up with the antics of Molefi. The tribal clerk was called Modibedi and he acted as the interpreter. He gave very flowery English versions of what was said in Setswana especially when the senior headman – Amos Pilane – spoke because Amos usually larded his contributions with

Tswana proverbs. Anyway I seemed to hit it off with Mmusi and the headmen and we fixed a date so I could be introduced to the tribe.

On the appointed day Modibedi telephoned from the tribal office to tell me the tribe was ready. When I arrived at the kgotla I was surprised by the size of the crowd. Mmusi must have issued a three line whip because there were nearly a thousand men waiting patiently most of them sitting on the ground and the more senior men on low locally made stools. Mmusi was waiting to greet me and escort me to the front to face the crowd and as one man they stood up in respectful silence. After Mmusi, the royal headmen and I had taken our seats the tribesmen resumed their sitting positions. Mmusi greeted the tribe and was answered by a loud throaty shout of "Kgabo" – Setswana for 'monkey', the totem animal of the Bakgatla. The shout echoed round the kopjes surrounding the kgotla. He then introduced me and said he was allocating me to the Lengope Mophato which is Setswana for the Donga Regiment. The Bakgatla were very traditional and still formed tribal regiments – that is males in age cohorts who could called upon by the chief to undertake certain communal tasks. In former times this would have also involved sending out young men to fight enemies. But Mmusi allocated me to a regiment mainly to indicate to the tribe how old I was. It was also his way of making me feel welcome. It remained a mystery to me how he had found out how old I was – he must have asked someone to find out for him.

I knew I was going to enjoy my time with the Bakgatla and I did. I quickly learnt not to trifle with them and never take short cuts with protocol. I was told about a rather arrogant Resident Commissioner who was persuaded to take a short cut to a village called Molepolole in the Bakwena Tribal Territory. He had to pass through a Bakgatla village on the way and going into this settlement posed no problem but getting out was more difficult because many tracks radiated out from it. After several dead ends and returns to start again he saw a man standing by the side of the track beside a bicycle from which he had dismounted. He told the chauffeur to stop and from the back seat of his official car asked the man in a rather querulous tone to point out the road to Molepolole. The Mokgatla, for that is what he was, told him he wasn't going to tell him. The irate official said " I am the Resident Commissioner" and accompanied this pronouncement by stabbing his finger at the Union Flag pennant fluttering on the front of the Pontiac. Completely unimpressed the Mokgatla replied that he knew the way to Molepolole and he wasn't going to tell him and mounting his bicycle rode off into the bush.

When the Resident Commissioner eventually reached Mole-polole and was having a soothing cup of tea on the verandah of the Residency he reported the incident to the District Commis-sioner and described where it had occurred. The District Commissioner listened politely and then respectfully pointed out that the Bakgatla expected people to greet them properly before firing questions at them. The Resident Commissioner was big enough to acknowledge his fault.

Although I got on very well with Mmusi working with him was not always easy. He managed to keep off the drink for long periods but every now and then he would go on a drinking spree. I always knew when he was starting one because when I called to see him he would be at his desk in his office with a large unopened bible in front of him and a tribal policemen in atten-dance. I knew that was the time to back off and wait for another day. He used to issue curious instructions when he was on a bender. For instance once when I went to the tribal offices to check on the accounts I was outraged to find that most of the staff were well in their cups. I sought out the Education Secretary, Francis Phiri, who was an upright, bespectacled, pillar of the church and a non-drinker. He told me that Mmusi had given orders that the staff must do their drinking in the middle of the day because drinking in the evening was keeping people in the village from their slumbers.

After these bouts he would make some gesture to indicate he was sorry. Once he gave me a cheetah skin. On another occasion he sent me a basket made by his then common law wife and this was accompanied by a charming letter composed no doubt by Modibedi which included a Setswana proverb to describe a meagre offering. When translated it read that parents did not reject wild spinach which had been collected for them by their small children simply because they had accidentally gathered weeds with it. On another occasion he informed me by letter that when Bridget and I had our first child he would call him "Mothusi" which means helper in Setswana. In the event our first child was a daughter born a couple of years after we left Mochudi but our Mokgatla servant Jane Selolwane who accompanied us frequently referred to her as Thusi.

A flogging

I hadn't been with the Bakgatla long when the Director of Veterinary Services came to see me with bad news. Foot and mouth disease had broken out in the Bamangwato territory on our northern border. This was serious because all cattle movements were suspended during such outbreaks so it was virtually impossible for the tribesmen to sell any stock. There was a disease control fence dividing the Bakgatla Territory from that of the Bamangwato but the Director said if a bush cordon were erected five miles south of the fence to form a buffer zone the chances of the disease spreading south would be greatly reduced.

I asked Mmusi to get the royal headman together and we had a meeting in his office at which I explained the situation. Mmusi immediately said he would call out a couple of regiments to put up the bush fence. I asked if he needed any help and he gave me to understand that this was a tribal matter and he and his uncles would attend to it. Work started on the fence within 24 hours.

About a week later the veterinary official supervising the work came to see me to report that the regiments were on strike and were demanding food and pay. Mmusi was very angry when I told him. He was all for going to tackle them with two or three of the tribal police and flogging the ringleaders but I said because they were doing work for government I would go and talk to the men. He agreed and told two of the royal headmen to go with me. He told me that had his brother Molefi been alive he would have gone up and flogged the lot but I said we would settle things a different way.

When we arrived at the regiments' camp I called the men together and we had a long meeting during which one individual – obviously a ringleader and a bit of a bush lawyer – questioned the right of anyone to require others to work without pay. We talked round and round the subject with the argumentative one becoming very heated and frequently interrupting me. Eventually the regimental leaders called on the men to make up their minds whether to continue with the work or remain idle and after a bit of muttering they began to get up and gather their axes and saws.

I was standing by my truck ready to get going back to Mochudi when the ringleader came and asked me to give him a lift back because he wanted to see the doctor. I told him to push off but one of the royal headmen intervened and told me to give the man a lift; he gave me an odd look that I didn't understand but I took his advice.

The next day just before noon I was in my office when a tribal policeman was ushered in. He had the tribal court register with him and told me through an interpreter that Mmusi wanted me to confirm a sentence that had been passed earlier that morning. I was intrigued and took the register. When I saw that I was being asked to confirm a sentence of flogging on the bush lawyer from the cordon fence, I immediately took off for the tribal offices – about two miles away. When I got there the sentence had already been carried out and the poor fellow was sitting on the steps to the offices looking very sorry for himself. I was very angry and took Mmusi and the royal headmen into the office and berated them. They knew I would not have approved of the sentence which was why they had sent the tribal policeman on foot to my office with the court register whilst they got on with the flogging. They remained completely unruffled at my scoldings and Mmusi said they could not allow anyone who had been so insolent to "their molaudi" – their District Commissioner – to get away with it.

Mochudi people

There were very few Europeans living in Mochudi apart from the government officials. The trader Johnny Odendaal had lived there for so long that he was almost a Mokgatla. Once the prisoners had been out collecting firewood in the veldt and they killed a huge python. They brought it back in triumph because they intended to feast off it but before they did they brought it round to the office to show me their trophy. They laid it out on the verandah and it must have been about 12 feet long. Later that afternoon I stopped at Johnny's store to make some purchase on my way to the tribal offices and told him about the python. Looking rather uneasy he told me not to tell *them* gesturing towards the tribal office because they believed it was unlucky to kill pythons at that time of the year (late October) because this drove away the rains and caused big dust storms.

That very night there was a huge dust storm that blew the roof off Johnny's store! I kept well out of his way for a few days after this and I think he harboured a grudge against me and my prisoners for a long time afterwards.

There was also a Coloured couple, Mr and Mrs Fritz, who ran a sort of bakery cum café. Their bread was pretty awful but it was the best available in the village until we learnt to bake our own. Mrs Fritz looked rather like a Red Indian squaw. I went to buy a loaf one day and was surprised by her appearance. She had a bandage wrapped tightly round her forehead with what looked like two stubby horns sticking out. She told me they were potatoes and their purpose was to cure her migraine by drawing out the pain.

A Jewish trader called Steinberg owned a trading store on the line of rail about two miles from the village. He was a big hearted and generous old man and a real pioneer. He came to Bechuanaland in the mid 1920s and I think he was from Estonia. In what I suppose was his living room behind the shop I noticed he had a picture taken from an old calendar of the view of Salisbury cathedral by Constable. What was unusual about this was that it was hung upside down. I don't think this represented his view of Christianity – he just hadn't noticed how his servant had replaced it after it had fallen down.

He could sign his name – just – but otherwise was illiterate yet he was an extremely shrewd businessman. His trusty assistant, Senoelo Sejoe, told me that when commercial travellers called and gave the old man some bit of promotional literature to read he would pat his pockets, claim that he must have mislaid his spectacles and call Senoelo over to read it for him. Once when he was ill he told Senoelo that he thought he was on his way out. Senoelo said "Don't die yet boss the ground is too hard to dig a grave" and this seemed to cheer him up no end.

Old Steinberg also owned a farm in a nearby European farming bloc that ran down to the South African border along the Marico river. He bought cattle from the tribesmen at his store and moved most of them to his farm to fatten them before selling them to the national abattoir or elsewhere. Many of them ended up being smuggled over the border where prices were usually higher. On one occasion a zealous young police sub-inspector who was determined to catch someone smuggling, counted the cattle on the farm and then returned two days later and said he proposed to count them again. The old man was alarmed because some of the cattle had been spirited away the previous night and were probably well on their way to the abattoirs in Zeerust and Rustenburg.

Anyway, resourceful as ever, he welcomed the fresh-faced young policeman and offered to help. He sent off his 'boys' to round up the cattle and gave the lad a table and chair so he could count in comfort. His 'boys' then whipped the cattle past the lad and he counted them. He found none missing and in fact an increase over the previous count. He departed after drinking a couple of Steinberg's beers with a packet of matzos given to him by his generous host. The old man gave his 'boys' extra rations because with their enthusiastic herding the young policeman had counted many of the cattle twice and some three times.

Life at the Residency

The Mochudi Residency was a fine old colonial building with large verandahs and a self contained guest wing. It was perched on the side of a kopje and commanded a fine view of the Notwani river flood plain. It was well supplied with fruit because when Eustace Clark was stationed there he installed an ingenious channel irrigation system for the orchard that was fed by the used bath water. The orchard consisted of pawpaw, guava, lemon, grapefruit and orange trees. In another part of the garden there was a magnificent grapevine. There was also a large swimming pool but it was difficult to keep the water clean as it had to be emptied by hand so we used it rarely and it was taken over by the geese we kept. The sitting room and dining room were lit by gas from cylinders stored outside so it was really quite luxurious and a change from paraffin lamps. We improved the garden tremendously with the help of a mason who was serving time in the prison for some offence. He built terraced walls and we planted shrubs and grass.

There was also quite a good tennis court adjoining the garden and the doctor at the Dutch Reformed Church mission asked whether he could use it and I agreed. He and his sons and daughters and a young white priest from the mission – the Rev Barry – began to use it. The Education Officer, Archie Mogwe, who was a keen tennis player, then joined the team of regular players. The Rev Barry had the nerve to approach me and say that he did not approve of playing sport with black people. I told him he had better play somewhere else if that was his view. The mission built their own tennis court soon after.

However the house had witnessed much sadness. The wife of a District Commissioner shot herself in the garden and the reason why was never discovered. Some years later a District Commissioner whose wife had left him for another man committed suicide by opening his veins in the bath. My first District Commissioner – Atters – told me that when he was stationed at Mochudi he had a lot of trouble with Chief Molefi. On one particular day when it was very hot, when his wife was away visiting relatives and when the chief was being particularly troublesome, he was lying in the bath when he began to think about the man who ended his life in that very place. So he quickly jumped out, dried himself, dressed and went for a walk up the kopje. He said that he discovered later that after the suicide the government turned the bathroom into an extension of the verandah and built on a new bathroom. I got the impression that he thought that had he succumbed to his gloomy thoughts he would have felt cheated!

We had a vegetable garden that was just as well as fresh vegetables were hard to get. The garden took a turn for the better when a prisoner arrived in the gaol from some over-crowded prison elsewhere and turned out to be a good gardener. However his reign in the garden was soon brought to an end. One of the station policemen was cycling through the village one day when he noticed a teenage boy who was wearing brand new overalls. The policeman knew the boy was penniless so he stopped him and asked where the overalls came from. The boy said his master had given him the money for them and named the convict gardener as the source of this bounty. The policeman discovered the boy was working for the prisoner selling vegetables in the village from my garden.

The prisoners in the Mochudi gaol had a fairly relaxed life. They collected firewood for the station and generally kept the little cantonment neat and tidy. There was no fence surrounding the prison and they usually relaxed round the fire much as they would have done at home. Most of them were in prison for rather petty offences. One however was in prison for raping a girl whilst she was having an epileptic fit but he was a cheerful chap. He used to chop the wood at the Residency and keep the outside boiler going. He was very popular with our servants and when he was released they gave him quite a send-off with a tin of condensed milk, a jar of jam and a bit of tea and sugar – all from our pantry I expect.

One Saturday afternoon we decided to try and buy a chicken

in the village to make a change from the rather monotonous beef, mutton and occasionally goat diet. We met a fellow I knew slightly and when I enquired about a chicken he insisted on giving me one of his as a present. I wasn't much good at wringing feathered necks so on the way home we stopped at the prison. The prisoners were relaxing round their fire and I asked the woodchopper to kill the bird for me. I remembered that we were going to use the giblets to make gravy so in my best Setswana I told him I particularly wanted the liver, heart, kidney and neck. We then retired to our afternoon siesta. Later I went to get a glass of cold water and saw the giblets neatly placed on a plate in the refrigerator but there was no sign of a chicken carcass. Fearing the worst I dashed off to the gaol to try and rescue our weekend treat but when I got there the prisoners seemed more relaxed than usual and there were several bones lying around. Bridget reckoned I had missed a chance. I should have said nothing and left them marvelling at my generosity.

We used to get our fair share of visitors at Mochudi because we were only about two miles from the main road that followed the line of rail up the country. I remember on one occasion a government official who was on his way north to attend some meeting connected with Moeng College that was in the Bamang-wato Tribal Territory called in for morning tea. It was a public holiday and as the offices were closed he came straight up to the Residency. We were sitting on the verandah waiting for the tea and I made some remark about the long and lonely journey ahead of him. He said he would not be lonely because he had company in the person of a schoolteacher from Kanye – a village in the south of the country. I asked where he was and was told he was waiting in the car. I went out and apologised to a rather slightly built man who was sitting quietly in the car that was parked in the shade of a large tree near the drive. I asked if he would like to join us for tea. It was Quett Masire who soon after gave up teaching to become Seretse Khama's deputy and eventually President of Botswana from 1980 to 1998. It was the beginning of a long and very precious friendship.

Dave Robinson

My district adjoined the Bamangwato Tribal Territory and in 1959 David Robinson who was a close friend – he was best man at my wedding in 1960 – was appointed District Commissioner in Serowe. The posting of Dave to Serowe was a brilliant move on the part of the Administration. He and Seretse Khama had been at Oxford together. Dave was a Trinity man and Seretse was at Balliol so this caused much friendly rivalry. They were both keen boxers. Dave was highly intelligent and a brilliant administrator. He had a marvellous sense of humour and was completely without prejudice.

Dave and I saw quite a bit of each other from time to time and through him I got to know Seretse at second hand as it were because since my meeting with him in Mahalapye way back in 1956 I had had very little direct contact with him. For several years he adopted a low profile and after his return from exile he had much work to do in attending to his private affairs. He had many cattle and although his trusty servants had looked after his interests in his absence he still had much to do to consolidate his holdings. He showed little interest in tribal and national affairs partly because he was inclined to be rather lazy and unambitious at that time but also because he was in very poor health.

Dave told me a story that Seretse had told him that illustrated perfectly Seretse's keen sense of humour. There was a clinic being built in Serowe by voluntary effort and a party of young people from the USA came out to lend a hand. As this was the first such visit by volunteers of this nature to Bechuanaland,

Seretse decided to go and meet them at Martin's Drift which was the post on the border with South Africa, and escort them to Serowe. The Sherwood Ranch hotel was a few miles from Martin's Drift and on the return journey Seretse decided to stop and have a drink. He was welcomed effusively by the proprietor Koos Alberts – a huge Afrikaner with a wall eye. Meanwhile the young Americans, some of whom were black, were swarming round the cool chest on the verandah that contained the soft drinks. When Koos spotted them he went out and asked them in his dog Setswana what they wanted. Their reply was heavily accented. On his return to the bar Koos, resting his elbows on the counter, thoughtfully surveyed the youngsters who were enjoying their Cokes and asked Seretse "What sort of language do these kaffirs speak, Chief?"

Another Seretse story that Dave told me amused me greatly. After lunch one Saturday in 1961 Dave's wife reminded him that they had been invited to a party that evening at the Khama's house. Dave then remembered it was Seretse's birthday and was annoyed that he had forgotten to buy him a present. Being a Saturday afternoon all the shops were closed so he couldn't rectify the omission. When dressing that evening however, he noticed he had a brand new Trinity tie in his drawer which was still in its cellophane wrapper so he made a parcel and took it along to the party. He gave the present to Seretse who was receiving guests at the door and when he had unwrapped it he made no comment and put it on the table. Dave thought his practical joke had fallen flat because Seretse did not appear to have recognised the colours of his rival college. The next morning Seretse telephoned Dave and invited him to come and have the hair of the dog. When Dave arrived at the closed gate of the Khama house a ragged young African boy ran out to open the gate wearing the inexpertly knotted Trinity tie. Seretse raised his glass in salute from the verandah.

David Robinson was just the right man to be stationed in Serowe at that time and he did much to encourage Seretse to become more involved in tribal affairs. This process was accelerated because Tshekedi died on 10 June 1959 and shortly after that Seretse succeeded him as Tribal Secretary. His stature as a future leader of the country began to emerge. He was influential in getting the Bamangwato tribe to surrender its claim to mineral royalties from mining within its territory and to regard them as national assets. He campaigned against the liquor laws that reserved 'white man's liquor' for whites and coloureds. A keynote speech he made to the Tribal Council about the need to remove discrimination from the laws of and practices in Bechuanaland led eventually to the Racial Discrimination Act which purged the Territory's laws of repulsive discriminatory provisions. In 1960 he met Quett Masire for the first time. They became firm friends and together they formed the Bechuanaland Democratic Party and set about planning the political future of the country. The BDP adopted Domkrag as its slogan. This is an Afrikaans word for a wagon jack and literally means silent power. The slogan was suggested probably by Quett Masire partly to suggest the unstoppable force of nationalism but also to mock Phillip Matante's strangulated pronunciation of Democratic – Matante was the leader of a rival party.

During these exciting times I was at Mochudi making steady progress in introducing more democratic forms of local government. But in early 1962 I was instructed to report to the Resident Commissioner in Mafikeng for consultations. I was mystified because I knew I hadn't blotted my copybook in any way and therefore was not being carpeted by the big man. I feared the worst and my fears were confirmed when I got there and was told I was being transferred to the Secretariat and was to report for duty within two weeks. The Resident Commissioner knew how happy I was in Mochudi because he had recently visited me there which was why he didn't just issue a posting order but called me down to break the news gently. When I returned to Mochudi and told Mmusi I would be leaving him he was very downcast. I too was sad to be leaving district work. I wondered why the people in Mafikeng couldn't just leave me alone and transfer whoever was going to replace me in Mochudi to Mafikeng but concluded that no doubt they had their reasons. Little did I realise then that I would never return to the districts but would become a headquarters man for the rest of my colonial career.

Top: Mochudi as it was in 1960.

Below: Chief Molefi of the Bakgatla, dressed for riding, with tribal elders in the kgotla in about 1937. Both photographs courtesy of Phutadikobo Museum, Mochudi.

Top: *Chief Molefi in RSM Uniform with the High Commissioner, Sir Evelyn Baring, at his re-instatement in 1945. Photograph by Senoelo Sejoe.*

Above: *Acting Chief Mmusi leaving the kgotla in about 1961. Both photograph courtesy of Phutadikobo Museum, Mochudi.*

David Robinson on leave in Oxford in 1962 two years before his tragic death in a road accident.

CHAPTER 8

TRANSFERRED TO HEADQUARTERS

Mafikeng is of course in the Republic (then the Union) of South Africa but by historical accident it was the capital of the Bechuanaland Protectorate or rather the Imperial Reserve was. This was on the edge of the town and several of the buildings that housed government officials had seen service when Baden Powell holed up there in 1900.

There was a sort of inner sanctum of offices that housed the Resident Commissioner and his administrative staff. These offices formed a square open on one side and grouped round a lawn with rose bushes and a tinkling fountain. It reminded me of a cloister in a cathedral close or the court of a Cambridge college. There was usually a deathly hush in the close and nobody to my recollection ever walked across the lawn except the black gardener. The offices were connected by little grey intercoms and one of the first tips I received was that you could ring sideways and down but never up. If you needed to consult a superior officer you got off your backside and went to see him in his office.

Other offices were scattered throughout the reserve and several of the more senior officers and their families were also housed there. But the majority of the people who worked in the headquarters lived in the town including, rather curiously, the Resident Commissioner who lived in the grandly named Protectorate House. I thought this was a very splendid residence but I was told that a Resident Commissioner in the early 1930s on being driven up to it when he took up his appointment thought it was the lodge to a much more imposing residence.

Coming from the bush we found Mafikeng very civilised. We were used to shopping at general dealers' stores but in Mafikeng there were specialist stores – chemists, butchers, greengrocers, cafés and tea rooms and clothing and shoe shops. There were a couple of prototype supermarkets and even a cinema. But in truth it was a very dreary town and in the dry season when the wind blew, dust storms swept over the heavily overgrazed neighbouring tribal areas and deposited their load everywhere. And of course being in South Africa racial discrimination was rampant.

I'm afraid that some of the headquarters officials who were employed in clerical cum junior executive capacities were racially biased and had little knowledge of and love for the Bechuanaland Protectorate. I well remember the tussle a couple of the other young Assistant Secretaries and I had with the office superintendent over the naming of a certain file. It was hilariously entitled Non Indigenous Natives and we had to stick to our guns to get the word 'Natives' replaced by 'Africans'.

Having the headquarters situated outside the Territory was a serious inconvenience but before the Nationalist Government secured its election victory in 1948 and consolidated it in 1953 there seemed to be an assumption in many quarters that the Protectorate would eventually become a province of South Africa.

However in 1962 when I was posted there, this was no longer on the cards and Bechuanland was on the move constitutionally which made the work in the Secretariat fascinating. Shortly after my arrival I was appointed clerk to the Executive Council and also clerk of the recently formed Legislative Council. Both of these Councils had been established in 1961 as a preliminary step to introducing more representative institutions.

Before 1961 Bechuanaland, along with Swaziland and Basutoland – the other two High Commission Territories – was uniquely politically backward amongst other British African dependencies. An African Advisory Council had been set up in 1919 and a European Advisory Council in 1920. In 1951 a Joint Advisory Council was created with eight members from each of the other councils. These bodies were consulted about proposed legislation but they were purely advisory and had no legislative functions.

My work with the recently established Legislative and Executive Councils brought me into frequent contact with Seretse Khama, Quett Masire and others who were to play key roles in the steps towards independence.

Headquarters work

The Legislative Council met in Lobatse partly because there was no suitable accommodation for it in Mafikeng and also to avoid possible embarrassment to the black members if they had to come to Mafikeng for meetings. In any event it would not have been possible for Seretse Khama to come to Mafikeng because he was a prohibited immigrant in South Africa simply because he was married to a white woman! The Council met in the High Court building and meetings were held about four times a year.

The Executive Council consisted of four government officials and four non-officials – two white and two black. Seretse Khama and Chief Bathoen represented African interests and Russell England (a trader) and David Morgan (an estate agent) European interests. The Resident Commissioner presided over this advisory body which met weekly in Lobatse in a government bungalow which had been set aside to provide office and refreshment facilities for the members of the Legislative Council.

These arrangements might appear to have been rather Heath Robinsonish but they worked very well. The standing orders of the budding legislative body were drafted with on-the-spot assistance by one of the Clerks in the House of Commons whose visit was followed by subsequent visits in future years by two of his colleagues. The procedure of the Executive Council was modelled on that of the British Cabinet. The work involved in servicing both of these bodies kept me rather busy but it was interesting being so closely involved in the political development of the country's institutions and I didn't mind the workload.

In true colonial service fashion the Resident Commissioner and his deputy didn't mind in the least adding to this workload from time to time. For instance the practice of issuing permits for guns and ammunition were grossly discriminatory. Europeans, Indians and Coloureds (people of mixed race) were entitled to import annually one rifle (other than a .303 or .22) and one shot gun and generous quantities of ammunition for them but Africans were virtually prohibited from importing or acquiring modern weapons. They were expected to make do with old Martini Henry rifles and other ancient firearms. Obviously this situation could not be allowed to continue and I was told to find a solution. To allow all and sundry to import what they liked would not have been in the best interests of the country and its wildlife. Eventually I produced a solution on a "need to possess" basis which seemed to satisfy all.

In the latter half of 1963 I was also told to take on the secretaryship of a committee that was planning the move of the headquarters and its staff from Mafikeng to Gaborone. This was very time consuming and one of my tasks was to prepare a detailed argument for funds to construct a dam near Gaborone to ensure water supplies to the future town – the Colonial Office had to be convinced that the town could hardly survive without adequate and assured water supplies! Eventually funds were granted rather reluctantly and I was told that one of the Colonial Office officials who handled the application thought it was full of "special pleading" but we didn't mind what he thought as long as we got the funds we needed.

Other odd jobs landed on my desk but I coped by getting to the office early and leaving late and, like most other officers in the Secretariat proper, I usually worked a seven day week but life was exciting and great fun.

Executive Council

Working with the Executive Council was particularly interesting and rewarding. Meetings were held every Wednesday except when the Legislative Council was in session when it met daily. The official members travelled to Lobatse from Mafikeng leaving fairly early in the morning and usually getting back to their offices by late afternoon. I used to try and have the minutes on the Government Secretary's desk before I left my office for the day but sometimes after a long meeting I could only manage this by mid-morning the next day.

I used to sit at a side table behind and to one side of the Resident Commissioner who presided with the Government Secretary on his right. The European non-officials sat on the Resident Commissioner's left and the African non-officials sat facing them. The official members occupied the other unreserved places round the table. From where I sat I had good eye contact with Seretse Khama.

Russell England was an interesting fellow. Someone told me he was German by birth but changed his name when he changed his nationality. My informant claimed to have seen on an application form for a passport that his name was originally Hoffenberg but I think this was a bit fanciful.

He was a thickset, almost bald, pipe-smoking man in his late sixties when I first got to know him. At one time he was Director of Agriculture but I believe he was almost totally unqualified for this post. He was very self-confident and must have been very energetic in his younger days. Anyway, he caught the eye of a Colonel Rey in the early 1930s – the Resident Commission associated with the Tshekedi incident when the marines got bogged down in the sand near Serowe. Rey promoted Russell England far beyond his qualifications and competence. However, he was very knowledgeable about the beef industry and was acknowledged as a sort of leader of white opinion in the Territory. But he wasn't very tactful and was inclined to pontificate. When he had delivered judgement he would emphasise whatever point he had made by ramming his pipe in his mouth and clenching it between his teeth so that it jutted out like a ship's bowsprit. Then he would sit staring ahead with his large head settled well down between his burly shoulders.

When the Legislative Council, of which he was a member, met in Lobatse, lunch was served in the house that government had set aside as the members' rest room. A local doctor's wife cooked for us. I thought she did rather well but Russell England, who was a great trencherman, thought the meals lacked substance. One morning he acquired several large fillet steaks from the local abattoir and handed them over to the amateur cook. When the Council adjourned for lunch he hastened to the bar and downed a large pink gin in eager anticipation of his steak meal. When he sat down and was served with bobotie – a Cape Malay dish consisting mainly of spiced minced meat – I thought he was about to attack the cook with his knife and fork.

He was a very good gardener. Once in Executive Council, under any other business, he said the nuns from a local convent school had told him the pupils taking the Cambridge Junior Certificate examination botany paper were required to draw a sweet pea from an actual specimen and had asked him if he had any such flowers in his garden. He asked the Resident Commissioner to write to the Colonial Office pointing out that such a requirement in the examination paper for pupils in Bechuanaland was ridiculous because, as it was winter in the Southern Hemisphere, it was impossible to get hold of specimens of sweet peas. He rounded off this request by adding "Africans don't like flowers anyway " and stuck his pipe back in his mouth. Chief Bathoen looked at the ceiling but Seretse caught my eye and said in a mild voice "But I rather like flowers Mr England".

On another occasion he had delivered one of his Olympian judgements and having identified to his satisfaction the cause of whatever was the trouble concluded by opining that it was "the nigger in the woodpile." I could tell by the way the Resident Commissioner's back stiffened that he hoped nobody would comment on this *faux pas*. In the silence that followed I caught Seretse's eye and he gave me a very slight wink. The Resident Commissioner glossed over the slip and wound up the meeting. After the meeting I was having a drink with Seretse at the bar and after a thoughtful silence he said "You know George, when I win this election and move into that house they are building for the Prime Minister in Gaborone I won't call it Chequers – I will call it 'The Woodpile'."

But these were amusing incidents in the serious business of the Council. It functioned very efficiently with memoranda being put to it for consideration and the decisions reached, recorded and transmitted for action to the embryonic "ministries" that had been established. We got through an enormous work schedule and the pace quickened at the end of 1963 when proposals for the granting of self government to Bechuanaland were published because in the run up to this profound constitutional change a considerable amount of legislation was needed.

Legislative Council

The Legislative Council at that time was composed of directly elected European members, African members chosen by the African Advisory Council acting as an electoral college and several official members. Despite its rather mongrel composition it operated very smoothly under standing orders modelled on those of the UK House of Commons.

One of the white members was an old man called Hendrick van Gass who represented the Tuli Block. He was a dyed in the wool Afrikaner nationalist and found it rather difficult to adapt to the new ways. One of his preoccupations was with stock theft and he was always calling for stiffer penalties to be imposed to stamp it out. Once in debate he was describing how thieves had cut his fences and stolen some of his best heifers and was struggling to find the word to describe the thieves. After spluttering "These – these – these" Seretse interjected "Kaffirs, Mr van Gass?"

On another occasion van Gass initiated a debate in the Council and proposed a motion inviting Dr Verwoed – the then South African Prime Minister – to address the Council on why the Tuli Block should be ceded to South Africa. A couple of days before the debate the old man had fractured his wrist whilst trying to start a borehole engine and he was quite clearly very unwell when he rose to speak. The Council dismissed the motion in scathing terms and van Gass withdrew. Outside the chamber later I was talking to Dr Bill Gemmill who as Director of Medical Services was one of the official members, when we saw van Gass getting into his car. Bill said that the old man was not long for this world and he was right.

Quett Masire was a great performer in the Legislative Council. He was a very good speaker and worked hard at mastering whatever subject was being debated. He much annoyed the officials of the Colonial Development Corporation when he mounted a vigorous attack on their management of the country's export abattoir. Quett formed a friendship with Bob Edwards, a young American recruited by the School of Public Administration at Syracuse University to work in the Secretariat and probably Bob provided him with much research material for his speeches.

Seretse spoke less in the Council but when he did he spoke with great authority. He was very laid back and some people thought he was not listening but he never missed a trick. Once a bill was being debated which had to do with raising finance in the form of a development loan from the UK for the construction of a dam in the south of the country. The dam was called the Nuane Dam and the official moving the bill pronounced these words several times with great precision during the debate. I caught Seretse's eye at some stage during the proceedings and it was obvious that something was amusing him.

Afterwards when we were having a drink in the bar I asked him what the joke was. He told me that "nuane" was the Setswana word for the female genitals. I leant later that when the surveyors were mapping the site for the dam they asked some young African herdsmen nearby the name of the valley and they told them. Apparently it got its name from a fold in the hills which resembled thighs!

Proposals concerning the constitutional future of Bechuana-land were made in a White Paper that was presented to Legislative Council in November 1963. In this Paper it was stated that a general election should be held in September or October 1964 if possible and in any case not later than the first quarter of 1965.

This was a rather tall order because although a census was underway nobody knew what the population of the country was so the task of delimiting constituencies would prove difficult. Further to this, elections were to be held on the basis of universal adult suffrage and the majority of the electorate was illiterate and had never voted in any election. When I read the proposals I remember thinking that Peter Fawcus, Her Majesty's Commissioner (the term Resident Commissioner had been abolished by then and replaced with this new title, often shortened to 'Queen's Commissioner') and his advisers had perhaps bitten off more than they could chew.

Top: African Advisory Council in 1946. Seated on the extreme right next to Chief Molefi is Forbes MacKenzie. 'Lawrie' Lawrenson is standing immediately behind him and on Lawrenson's right is Norman Mathews.

Below: ceremonial opening of African Advisory Council in Mafikeng in 1947. Photographs supplied by Noel Redman.

Right: Tsheko Tsheko, with GW behind, at the Food and Agriculture Organisation meeting in 1967.

Below: GW receiving the MBE from Sir Hugh Norman Walker, Queen's Commissioner, in 1966.

CHAPTER 9

THE FIRST ELECTIONS AND MOVING THE CAPITAL

The White Paper on the constitutional proposals was laid before the Legislative Council in November 1963. Late one afternoon shortly after this Arthur Douglas, the Chief Secretary, (by then this title had replaced that of Government Secretary) stalked into my office and dumped an enormous pile of reports on my desk and said "How to organise an election." He advised me to read them carefully because they were all about elections in other countries in Africa and it had been decided that I would be in charge of the arrangements for the forthcoming elections in Bechuanaland. He said nothing about relieving me of some of my other duties and of course I didn't make such an outrageous suggestion so I was left contemplating a very busy year ahead.

Organising these elections was a daunting task. Although a census was underway the preliminary results on which detailed planning could proceed would not be available until the middle of 1964. Then the country had to be divided into constituencies so that the registration of voters could take place at the 300 or so polling stations and everything had to be ready so that voting could take place between 6 a.m. and 6 p.m. on 1 March 1965. Making these arrangements in a country 12,000 square miles bigger than France with only about 2 miles of tarred roads was quite a challenge.

The Democratic Party led by Seretse Khama and Quett Masire was so well organised that it was obvious from the outset that it would win the election especially as the opposition had split into three parties and was more or less in disarray. This made it essential that the arrangements for the elections had to be above reproach because allegations of rigging the vote in favour of Seretse by the British administration would be made. In fact no matter how fair the arrangements were such allegations would almost certainly be made. To begin the fairness campaign I offered to provide each party with 500 election posters bearing the party slogan. One of the parties submitted its slogan as "One man one vote regardless of sex" but I persuaded the leader to change it so as to avoid possible ridicule.

But the most important aspect was devising a voting system suitable for a largely illiterate population. In some countries the 'whispering vote' had been adopted by which the presiding officer took the voter into the polling booth and marked the ballot paper according to his or her whispered instructions. This was quite obviously out because it would attract allegations of vote rigging. Another important factor that was taken into account was that many illiterate people are unable to handle a pen or pencil so even making a cross could prove beyond them even if they could read the names of the candidates on the ballot paper.

After much thought I asked the parties to adopt a colour and a symbol for campaign purposes. When people came to vote they were then given as many coloured cardboard discs as there were candidates for election and told to go into the polling booth, put the colour of their choice in an envelope, seal it, put it in the ballot box and discard the unwanted discs in a discard box. Before launching this system on the country at large I tested it on the prisoners in the Lobatse gaol and it worked perfectly as it did at the general election in March 1965.

Another matter that exercised my mind for many days was how we could provide polling booths at the 300 plus polling stations. To distribute portable booths over the vast area of

Bechuanaland would have been a formidable task and would have been very expensive. But we had to have polling booths so constructed to preserve the secrecy of the ballot. I finally decided that each polling station would be issued with four 6 ft poles, a ball of twine, drawing pins and a length of sacking. A perfectly satisfactory polling booth could be constructed by lashing the poles to the legs of a table and pinning the sacking to these poles leaving one side open. A very simple solution to what seemed an intractable problem!

However in early 1964 whilst the planning of the elections was under way we had a tremendous shock. Seretse Khama became very seriously ill and was rushed to hospital in Bulawayo. Quett Masire stood in for him on the Executive Council. On 19 February, just before midday when the Council was in session we heard footsteps pounding down the corridor to the meeting room and the proceedings were interrupted by a loud knocking on the door. It was the OC Police of the Lobatse station – Chips Knight – who reported in a loud voice that he had received a message from Bulawayo that Seretse Khama had died earlier that morning in hospital.

Everyone froze. When the Queen's Commissioner Peter Fawcus recovered himself he asked the Chief Secretary Arthur Douglas to carry on whilst he made further enquiries and he left the room. Quett Masire, numb with shock, sat crumpled in his chair staring at the papers in front of him his face a picture of blank misery. I wondered what thoughts were swirling through his mind. The unflappable Arthur Douglas, filling his pipe, said he thought we should get on with the meeting and await further news that might be other than what we had just heard. I don't think Quett paid any attention to what was discussed after this interruption. However, we had just finished the meeting when the Queen's Commissioner returned and said he had spoken to the hospital administrator. Seretse was still very ill but comfortable. Everyone visibly relaxed and Quett's face reflected his enormous relief.

After this scare planning for the future elections and the setting up of the other arrangements for internal self-government proceeded apace but on 3 June we received devastating news. On the afternoon of that day Jimmy Allison who was standing in for the Chief Secretary who was on leave, called me to his office. When I went in he was sitting with his head in his hands. He looked up, motioned to me to be seated and gazed at me for a few moments without saying a word. Then he picked up a telegram from the desk and pushed it towards me before getting up to stare out of the window. I picked up the telegram and when I had read it I sat frozen with shock and grief. It was from the Colonial Office in London informing us that Dave Robinson had been killed the day before in a motor accident. I didn't want to believe it. He was such a fine man and a very good friend. It was so cruel that a brilliant career had been cut short. His wife Judy nursed their little daughter in hospital. She had been in the car with her father and her grandmother – who was also killed – but the child died a few days later. Thankfully their baby son, who had been in the following car with his mother and grandfather, survived.

More bad news was to follow. Later that year Quett Masire was hospitalised for several weeks suffering from chemical poisoning. When he awoke one morning after a trip to Mafikeng the previous day he felt distinctly unwell and decided to stay in bed. His condition deteriorated and the Seventh Day Adventist mission doctor was called in. He was very puzzled and said he thought the symptoms were of some sort of poisoning. Quett immediately remembered that he had bought some pesticide in Mafikeng for use on his cotton crop and he had carried it home in a suitcase containing his pyjamas and other clothing. The longer he stayed in bed the more poison he absorbed from his contaminated pyjamas and he had absorbed enough to require specialist medical attention which was not available in Bechuanaland at that time. Thankfully he recovered sufficiently to carry on running the campaign for his party but I think he would have preferred and benefited from a longer convalescence.

This was a very busy period indeed for the team manning the Secretariat in Mafikeng. The legislative programme was very heavy. A census of the territory was under way. A Delimitation Commission was deciding on the future constituencies. A countrywide registration of voters was being planned and seven information teams were touring the country preparing the population for the elections. Added to this activity plans to move the headquarters lock stock and barrel from Mafikeng to Gaborone about 100 miles north were well under way. From the middle to the end of 1964 the new capital began to emerge from the bush between the railway station and the old government camp that became known as Gaborone village.

The main move of the administration from Mafikeng to Gaborone took place between 5 February and 20 February 1965. This was brilliantly planned by Peter Heady, an adminstrative officer in the Secretariat. The Secretariat files were moved over one weekend.

Pantechnicons rolled up dead on time on the appointed day and officers' house contents were loaded on them before they set off in convoy up the dirt road to the north. I seem to remember that I missed only one day in the office whilst my wife and I settled in to our new bungalow on the North Ring Road of the new capital together with our eight month old daughter and our three dogs. It was an exhilarating experience. It didn't seem to matter that there were few shops, that the electricity failed from time to time and many buildings were still under construction. It seemed like a brave new world. Our bungalow was fenced and even though the "garden" was raw bush we could already visualise what it would become. I didn't mind in the slightest leaving Mafikeng behind because we now had our own capital in our own country and at long last Bechuanaland was well on the road to self government under its own Prime Minister.

I had to return to Mafikeng however because I had left all the elections paraphenalia there and had arranged for fleets of lorries to start distributing the equipment needed for the election to the polling stations. Packing this equipment was a demanding task. I had ordered about 400 hundred large wooden egg crates that were packed and labelled according to polling stations. The slightest omission of almost any item of equipment could spell disaster on polling day because just about each item was essential for the success of the election. So the boxes were packed with great care – the correct number of voting discs and of posters, the correct voters' roll for the polling station, sellotape, drawing pins, sealing wax, envelopes, ball point pens and many other items which presiding officers would need. After each box had been packed a separate team checked its contents before it was put in its correct place according to constituency in the room set aside as a loading bay.

During the months preceeding the election date I had selected and trained the registration officers and the presiding and polling officers needed and they had all been issued with detailed written instructions. The co-operation was excellent in general. Some truculent individuals who were not all that keen on handing over the reins of government attempted to get out of election duties but their heads of department soon whipped them into line and I rewarded their lack of enthusiasm by assigning them to remote polling stations.

By the beginning of the third week in February the boxes of polling equipment and the polling booth bundles were all under the care of the returning officers of the constituencies ready for collection by the presiding officers of the various polling stations over the weekend preceding Monday 1 March which was polling day. All I could do was to wait and hope that nothing had been overlooked.

At about 4 a.m. on the morning of 1 March I woke after a bad dream. I dreamt that the election had been a complete flop and few people had turned up to vote at the polling stations in the outside villages. I was up soon after five and visited the polling station at Ootsi, a village south of Gaborone. When I rounded a corner in the track leading to the school that was being used as a polling station I was much relieved to see a queue a couple of hundred yards long waiting to vote. Several officers who had to leave very early in the morning to get to their polling station before 6 a.m. told me later that it was eerie travelling along the bush tracks because people were everywhere like ants streaming to the polling stations.

And so the first general election in Bechuanaland was a resounding success. The presiding officers did a wonderful job and made sure that everything was done according to the book. The results came in slowly at first but by the middle of the afternoon of 2 March it was clear that Seretse Khama's Democratic Party had won a resounding victory. The final tally was Bechuanaland Democratic Party 28 seats and the Bechuanaland People's Party three seats. The other parties failed to get any members elected.

The new government

So Seretse Khama was sworn in as Prime Minister and Quett Masire became his deputy. All the other ministers, Ben Thema, Amos Dambe, Tsheko Tsheko, Englishman Kgabo, Mout

Nwako, Archie Tsoebebe were all well known to me and it was marvellous to see them assembled in Cabinet.

Shortly after the election Sir Peter Fawcus, Her Majesty's Commissioner announced his retirement. He had not been very well for some months but he never allowed this to interfere with his driving force to set Bechuanaland on the road to self government. However I think the main reason for his deciding to go was that having been such a dominant and moving figure in the country's constitutional advancement he wanted to make room for Seretse to develop his own style of government. It is also possible that he wanted to make room at the top for his deputy Arthur Douglas. Sadly this was not to be and Hugh Norman Walker was sworn in as the new Queen's Commissioner on 16 July 1965.

During this time I was working in the Prime Minister's Office as Clerk to the Cabinet. I know that Setetse was very disappointed that Arthur Douglas had not been appointed to succeed Peter Fawcus and he found it very difficult to get on with Norman Walker – their relationship didn't prosper after Norman Walker's black labrador cross – Casca by name – bit Seretse at one of his early meetings with the new Queen's Commissioner in his office. Thereafter whenever he went to meetings and the dog was around Norman Walker would lock the beast in the lavatory from where it howled its disapproval of being prevented from taking another chunk out of the new Prime Minister.

It was great working with Seretse. When he was around he always popped in to my office for a few words each morning whilst on his way to his office. He often had a piece of biltong for me or a piece of pani – dried mophane worm, a great delicacy amongst the Batswana. He knew what was going on in Gaborone and he must have had a wonderful intelligence network. For instance one of the African civil servants had words with me one evening at the new hotel in town because I said I wasn't going to some dance that was being held nearby. He said I was afraid that some black man would dance with my wife. I told him not to be so childish. A couple of mornings later Seretse, whilst perched on the radiator in my office, mentioned this slight altercation and said he supposed the truth was that like him I didn't much enjoy dancing which was exactly right. On another occasion when we were chatting my secretary came in with some papers. She greeted him in some confusion and after she had left he asked me if I knew who she was. I replied that of course I did – she was my secretary. He replied rather acidly that apart from that she was his cousin.

The Permanent Secretary to the Prime Minister was my old friend Jimmy Allison – a most conscientious and hard working man. He became very worried because Seretse was not attending to his paper work and the files were piling up on the prime ministerial desk. Jimmy expected Seretse to fall in with the usual civil service means of communicating by writing long minutes to each other. I told Jimmy he had better forget that and just go and talk to Seretse and get his nod or otherwise to whatever particular problem was bothering him but I could see Jimmy was uneasy. Shortly after this exchange of views Jimmy went off on a couple of days break and in the space of a couple of hours I demolished the file mountain with Seretse's help. He was the sort of man who would never let you down – his word was better than a dozen minutes on file.

I remember once asking Seretse if he would help in choosing a set of designs for a stamp series to be issued by the Crown Agents to commemorate Bechuanaland's attainment of self gov-ernment. The theme suggested was of Batswana troops in the 1939-45 war and a selection of photographs had been supplied by the Crown Agents. One of them was of Batswana troops loading sacks of flour or something on to an aeroplane and I remarked that I thought it was unsuitable. Seretse said he thought it was a good photograph so what was wrong with it? I said it showed the Batswana in a labouring light. He told me not to be so sensitive – "somebody has to load the 'plane".

The only person I ever heard him talk about unkindly was Patrick Gordon Walker. He loathed the man mainly because when he was Colonial Secretary and Seretse was in conflict with the Colonial Office over his marriage and the chieftainship issue, Gordon Walker advised him to go back to Bechuanaland and she [Ruth] "would soon find another chap." Seretse never forgot this appalling insult and told me how delighted he and Ruth were when Gordon Walker not only lost his seat in the 1951 UK general election but went on to lose a 'safe' Labour seat in a manufactured subsequent bye election. I sometimes wondered whether he didn't take to Norman Walker because his name was so like that of his old adversary.

When Seretse became Prime Minister Sir Peter Fawcus continued to preside over Cabinet meetings and when he retired Norman Walker assumed this role. Seretse found this particularly irksome. He just couldn't get on with Norman Walker's loud, rather swaggering style that was very different from the patient, quiet courtesy of his predecessor. Once when I was taking the minutes at some meeting concerning the future independence constitution attended by Seretse, Quett, Norman Walker, Arthur Douglas and Alan Tilbury (the Attorney General) Norman Walker made some intervention prefaced by saying that he was "speaking as a financial chap." Seretse passed a scrap of paper down to me on which he had scribbled "Speaking as a financial chap!!!" I bobbed my head, crumpled the note and shoved it in my pocket. After the meeting Arthur Douglas cornered me and asked "What was in the note that the Prime Minister passed to you?" I said he wanted to know whether I had any biltong. Arthur smiled. I don't think he believed me.

However the powers of the office of the Queen's Commissioner gradually diminished and the Prime Minister's office began to take on more and more responsibility. In September 1965 Seretse was given power by a British Order-in-Council to preside over Cabinet meetings and I think we were all very relieved. Seretse was a very good chairman. David Finlay, his Private Secretary, bequeathed to him by Peter Fawcus, made sure he was very well briefed and he handled the meetings with despatch but with great patience when some minister was being rather tedious. His good humour was never far below the surface. Once when a rather naughty minister pitched up wearing large sunglasses to hide a shiner given to him by an irate husband, Seretse made a point of admiring the new sunglasses.

The Ministers and I used to assemble outside the Cabinet room to await the arrival of Seretse who would be accompanied by his Permanent Secretary. One of the ministers was irritated by Seretse's insistence that suits had to be worn at Cabinet meetings and said he proposed to raise the issue under any other business. He had recently returned from an official visit to Germany and was wearing a rather curious German suit that had about eight buttons up the front. I used to meet Seretse's car when he came to meetings and as he was getting out he asked me what "they" were up to now. I passed on the any other business matter about suits or non suits. When we had finished the formal agenda Seretse asked for any other items and the minister who thought shorts and open neck shirts were suitable for Cabinet meetings said he thought ministers should come to Cabinet "properly dressed." Seretse leaned back in his chair, studied the minister for some moments, then slowly ran his eyes round the other ministers before saying "But who is improperly dressed Mr xxxx, apart that is from yourself?" The subject was never raised again.

Moving towards Independence

During Bechuanaland's first few months of self-government the constitutional wrangle between the UK and Southern Rhodesia reached its fateful conclusion and on 11 November 1965 the latter country made its illegal declaration of independence. Many of the white residents in the north of Bechuanaland and of Francistown in particular applauded this move and regarded it as a plucky show of defiance by Rhodesians of left wing politicians in the UK. Race relations in Francistown were poor and the opposition party (the Bechuanaland People's Party) made much of this and it was probably his skilful exploitation of the issue which resulted in Phillip Matante's success in winning a Francistown seat in the 1965 election.

Race relations were such that when an Egyptian doctor who was a good tennis player expressed his desire to join the Francistown Club so that he could pursue his interest in the game, a special meeting of the club committee under its hard line president met in emergency session to 'tidy up' the constitution. The result was that the constitution was amended to make it clear that membership was restricted to whites only. This was a foolish act. The government could have taken any number of legislative actions to make it difficult if not impossible for the club to continue to operate under its offensive constitution.

However, as even handed as ever, Seretse moved cautiously. The chairman of the Francistown Club was manager of the local branch of the Witwatersrand Native Labour Association (WNLA) that recruited labourers for work in the South African gold mines. Seretse invited the General Manager of WNLA who was based in Johannesburg to come to Gaborone to discuss the antics of his employee – not to try to enforce disciplinary action but to make clear his profound displeasure. In the end this softly softly approach paid off. The matter of the Francistown Club proved a nine days wonder and eventually it withered on the vine. The same happened to the Gaborone Sports Club which was never overtly anti-black although there were no black members. It was simply eclipsed when the Notwani Club, open to all races, was formed.

However these matters were not allowed to impede Bechuanaland's smooth progress towards independence. Early on it was decided that there should not be a prolonged period between internal self-government and independence as this could lead to uncertainty and there was no good reason for unduly delaying the inevitable. There were many matters to be settled before this desirable end to colonial status could be brought about. Complicated constitutional and financial consultations were set in train. These were outside my field of competence but I became much involved in selecting a national anthem and in the design of the coat of arms and flag.

It was decided to hold competitions for all three to try and involve the population at large. I issued the necessary notices and received several entries for each category – one application was from a Standard Six pupil who said he "was hereby applying for the position of the coat of arms or the national anthem or the flag".

The leader of one of the failed opposition parties in the general election – K.T. Motsete – a man with many academic degrees including one in music, submitted an early entry for the national anthem competition. Others followed but they did not match Motsete's. Seretse was keen to have *Kgosi Segofatsa Afrika* as the anthem but I urged him to chose one which could be Botswana's own – I even told him Kgosi Segofatsa had been chosen by Tanzania – I'm not sure that I was correct. In the end Seretse agreed we should have a concert in Gaborone at which all the entries would be performed and we would make a final choice. We did and Motsete's entry was chosen. We needed an English version of the words and Mokgwadi Kgopo, a senior civil servant, made a literal translation of the words as submitted by Motsete and I got my father-in-law to make this translation more poetic.

The entries we received in the flag competition were hopeless so I designed the flag myself. I wanted to make it easy to draw hence the straight all horizontal lines. The blue background of the flag represents water – vital to the country's agriculture – and the black central strip bordered with two white strips represents racial harmony.

The coat of arms proved more difficult. We received two good entries, one from Lady Fawcus and one from Lady England. However the Cabinet decided that neither was suitable as it stood and asked me to arrange for the best in both to be combined. My wife made the sketch as directed and after Cabinet approval this was submitted to the College of Heralds in the UK who made more alterations and produced a final design. The two zebra symbolise the abundant wildlife in the country as well as alluding to black/white co-operation, the ivory tusk also refers to the wild life, the ox head and the stalk of sorghum refer to the agricultural resources, the interlocking cogwheels suggest the mineral potential and the wavy blue lines emphasise the importance of water in an arid country such as Botswana. The supporting word PULA – the Setswana word for rain – suggests happiness and optimism.

The run-up to independence was smooth. Much hard work was put into creating the gardens between the four principal ministerial office blocks. I was horrified to see a couple of Public Works Department graders arrive on the scene to begin clearing the bush between the blocks. I rustled up Peter Harrison the Senior Architect and together we marked the trees that were to stay and those that could be cleared. The Director of Veterinary Services arranged for several truck loads of well rotted manure to be collected from the cattle quarantine camps and spread around the potential gardens and the Director of Water Affairs arranged for a sprinkler system to be installed. I recruited the voluntary services of Jean Posthumus, the wife of the Deputy Director of Veterinary services and a very good gardener, to lay out the flowerbeds. Soon the whole area began to take shape.

The National Assembly buildings which formed the focal point of the ministerial blocks were under construction whilst all this work was going on and, whilst it was clear that they would be completed in time for the independence ceremony at which Princess Marina would represent the Queen, it was apparent that there would be no time to establish lawns and flower beds to conceal the raw earth. I contacted a local farmer's wife, Rita Brink, who had a marvellous garden at her farmhouse near Gaborone. Rita said we should create "lawns" by planting millet seed very thickly and watering it so the green shoots would be a couple of inches high on independence day and she would transplant flowering plants from her garden a day or two before the ceremonies so all would look presentable. She took charge and the instant garden was a credit to her.

I was put in charge of the seating arrangements in the public gallery of the chamber for the official guests and I had to arrange this with great care so that the representatives of countries unfriendly to each other were kept apart. I marked the guests' names on the seats with labels. I used white labels at first but these ran out and not having any more of that colour I switched to red, reasoning that once the guests were seated nobody would see the labels.

Independence

The Independence celebrations began on the evening of 29 September. The day had been warm and promising but about 6 o'clock that evening a wind began to rise and by 11 was roaring about Gaborone at almost gale force. Princess Marina and the Khamas put on a brave face, wrapped themselves warmly and took their seats in the newly erected stadium just before midnight. The Union Flag was lowered for the last time and the new Botswana flag was unfurled. It proved rather obstinate at first but after a few tugs on the rope was soon fluttering proudly in the stiff wind. Many expatriates told me later how sad they were to see the Union Flag being lowered but I felt no sadness at all. All I felt was pride that Bechuanaland had come so far and was now the independent Republic of Botswana.

I was up early on the day after the independence ceremony in the stadium and went to check that all was in order at the parliamentary buildings. Standing beside the Speaker's chair that had been transformed into a temporary throne, I ran my eyes over the public gallery and was surprised to see a red label amongst the white labels I had used to allocate places. I went to investigate and found that someone had moved the label for the Foreign Minister of South Africa and put it between seats assigned to delegates from two independent African states. I put matters right and decided to avoid any trouble by saying nothing about it to anyone.

After the independence celebrations in Gaborone were over the government arranged for the Princess Marina and her party to take a short break in the Chobe Game Reserve in the north of the country. John Sheppard, a Botswana Special Branch officer, was instructed to liaise with the Princess' bodyguards and to accompany the party. He told me that after dinner on the first evening the Princess decided to have an early night. After those detailed to watch over her had seen her safely installed in her bedroom in the Chobe Hotel they relaxed with a drink just outside the door of the corridor leading to her room. John said they were chatting quietly over their drinks when a loud scream from the Princess' bedroom brought them to their feet. Her bodyguard turned pale and hurled himself down the corridor in the direction of the bedroom. He was closely followed by John who witnessed him comforting the Princess who, draped in a bath towel and wearing a shower cap, was staring wide eyed at a huge, hairy rain spider in the shower tray. It was of little comfort to her to be told that the creature was absolutely harmless. The spider was removed and everyone relaxed.

After the excitement of the independence celebrations life returned to normal. We had to move offices because Seretse who was now President had moved into State House and his office suite was close to it. Meetings of the Cabinet were now held in a magnificent suite of rooms in the National Assembly buildings and Seretse continued to preside over them with dignity and authority. I much enjoyed being so close to the seat of power and watching the ministers develop the authority of their respective offices.

Right: Tsheko Tsheko talking to herdsmen trekking cattle from Ghanzi to the abattoir at Lobatse.

Below: Quett (later Sir Ketumile) Masire, greeting visitors to the Independence celebrations, 1966. Photograph by Noel Redman.

Right: Sir Seretse Khama, HRH the Princess Marina, Sir Hugh Norman Walker and Lady Khama gathered for Independence ceremonies in 1966.

Right: HRH the Princess Marina and Sir Seretse Khama at the Independence Ball in 1966.

CHAPTER 10

THE MINISTRY OF AGRICULTURE

A few months after independence Jimmy Allison, who was still Permanent Secretary to the President, came into my office and told me in confidence that a vacancy would arise soon in the Ministry of Agriculture because the serving Permanent Secretary was leaving the service on retirement and Seretse had hinted to Jimmy that he wanted me to succeed him – just a hint because he, Seretse, did not want to interfere in Civil Service appointments. I was delighted because apart from the promotion involved, working in the Ministry of Agriculture would bring me in close touch with the people in the districts who depended on agriculture for their livelihood. However, my hopes were dashed later in the day when Jimmy told me that he had blundered because there was an expatriate officer senior to me in the Civil Service list and he would have to be appointed to the post. The next day Jimmy called me in and said he was in deep trouble because Seretse had made it clear to him that he wasn't much interested in Civil Service lists and he wanted me in Agriculture. Jimmy was under the impression that because the number of Ministers was laid down in the constitution the number of Permanent Secretaries was also limited. I suggested he consulted the Attorney General which he did and was told that there was no constitutional limit to the number of Permanent Secretaries who could be appointed.

And so I got the Ministry I wanted. I also got the Minister I wanted in the person of Tsheko Tsheko, my old friend from Maun days. He was as good a minister as he had been Tribal Secretary – quiet, courteous and efficient. I used to marvel at his desk which was always clear of papers except those on which he was currently working.

The Assistant Minister was a Mokgatla by the name of R.D. Molefe. I was a bit apprehensive about how he would react to my appointment because when I was District Commissioner at Mochudi and Chairman of the Bakgatla Schools Committee I had been instrumental in having him removed from the headmastership of a school for poor performance. However, he was a bigger man than I had given him credit for and he welcomed me. My principal difficulty with him was to stop him addressing me as "Sir".

Shortly after my appointment we received some papers from the Establishments Office concerning the recruitment of a young Englishman who had applied for the post of Agricultural Officer that had been advertised. The UK authorities had warned us that he had been deported from Tanzania. I read the papers and went to discuss the matter with Tsheko Tsheko. The young chap in question had spent several months organising a farmers' day in his district. A couple of days before the jamboree was due to take place he had visited Dar es Salaam on business but had been hauled into the Ministry and told he would have to cancel his farmers' day because the President would be making a tour of his district at that time. Exasperated, he said "Oh bugger the President." or words to that effect. He was on his way home to the UK a few days later.

Tsheko Tsheko listened carefully then looking down at the papers in front of him and thinking the matter over for a few moments looked up at me and cocking his head on one side said "I think we do things differently here George."

I frequently marvelled at the ability of the Batswana to rise above whatever indignities had been heaped upon them in the past and remain courteous and smiling to those who had been, and in many cases still were, their superior officers. They were remarkably tolerant of the failings in others and no doubt many took their lead from their President.

A good example of toleration involved Quett Masire when he was the Vice President. He wanted to discuss something with me one evening and decided to call in on his way to the hospital to visit a sick relative. Unknown to him I had moved house and when he drew up outside where he thought I still lived he saw a car which was not mine in the drive. Thinking I had visitors he decided to call on his way back from the hospital.

When he returned the strange car was still parked in the drive so he decided to seek me out. A very unfriendly man who was a senior expatriate government official answered his knocking and aggressively demanded to know what he wanted. When Quett asked for me he was told I had moved and the aggressive one didn't know where. Quett asked for the official's telephone number and was about to be told to mind his own business when the woman of the house appeared and pushing her rather intoxicated husband to one side disclosed their number. Quett said that in that case I must have transferred my number to my new residence and asked if he could use their telephone to contact me. The woman ushered him in and he rang me. I was on the lawn beside the swimming pool of my new house and took time to answer the ringing. Whilst he was waiting for me to reply the aggressive one appeared again and thrust his face close to Quett's. He snarled that Quett should just go and find me and stop intruding on him when I picked up my telephone. Quett said "Hello George, this is Quett Masire." His unwilling host recognised the name and Quett told me he watched the expression on the face before him change from angry indignation to one of "Oh my God what have I done now".

The official in question contacted me the next morning and gave me a garbled account of the incident. That evening I attended a reception and Quett was present. I asked him what had happened the previous evening and he gave me the account as detailed above. An expatriate Permanent Secretary who was listening to our conversation interjected with words to the effect that Ministers should take steps to make themselves better known then members of the public would recognise them. Quett replied very acidly that he did not expect to be always treated as the Vice President but he did expect to be treated like a human being. When I asked him later whether he wished to pursue the matter he said we should leave it and hope that the man in question had learned his lesson.

Quett had a great sense of humour and I saw this vividly demonstrated once at a ceremony involving the handing over of several Africander bulls to the Ministry of Agriculture by the Africander Breeders' Association of South Africa. The acceptance of this gift had been cleared by our Cabinet and on the appointed day Tsheko Tsheko, Quett Masire and several black and white officials gathered on a Government-owned farm near Lobatse to receive the bulls and the accompanying party. We were surprised to discover that Jim Fouche, President of the Republic of South Africa, was a member of the party – I think he was a keen breeder of Africander cattle. Everything went well and the appropriate speeches were made. Quett had to leave early because he had business to attend to in Gaborone so he approached Jim Fouche to say farewell. He acted the part of a down trodden black in South Africa, his body half bowed from the waist and with one hand covering an ear said "Baie baie dankie my basie" ("Thank you, thank you, my boss"). Jim Fouche who was quite a humorous fellow looked surprised but quickly recovered and replied addressing him as "My kaffertjie". Quett roared his approval of the riposte which was also much appreciated by the other Batswana who had witnessed the exchange.

In the middle of 1968 we learned that President Kaunda was planning a state visit to Botswana in August of that year and apparently the proposed programme for his visit was discussed in Cabinet. Naturally I no longer attended Cabinet meetings and when Tsheko Tsheko returned to his office he called me in and said that he had offered to organise an agricultural show in Gaborone as part of the programme for the state visit. I was aghast because organising such a show at very short notice required consider-able effort and a large slice of luck if it were to be successful. Jimmy Allison who as Senior Permanent Secretary attended Cabinet meetings said that when Tsheko Tsheko had made the offer Seretse and other Ministers had queried whether such a show could be organised in such a short time and he had simply replied "George will do it."

After my meeting with the Minister I called in the heads of departments and broke the news to them. They were marvellous and the feeling was that "we must not let the Minister down." Everyone got stuck in and the show was one of the highlights of the state visit. Both Seretse and Kaunda were farmers at heart and we had some magnificent cattle to show them.

Later in 1968 there was a conference at Mbarara in Uganda to do with settlement of farmers on freehold beef farms. Tsheko Tsheko and I were interested in this because we wanted to introduce individual tenure for Africans in selected parts of Botswana so we decided to attend. When Quett heard about the conference he decided to come to because he was very interested in the subject. We flew by BOAC to Entebbe and just before we landed were instructed over the loudspeaker to remain seated when we landed because important Ugandan officials were coming on board. We did as instructed and I noticed much activity going on in the first class. I asked one of the stewards what was happening and was told they were looking for the Vice President and the Minister of Agriculture from Botswana and I said they were sitting next to me. The Ugandans hauled us off the plane to a red carpet and a huge champagne reception in the VIP lounge. They were amazed that Botswana ministers should travel economy class. Some years previously when Quett was deputy Prime Minister I had drawn his attention to the large difference between first and second class air fares and he had decided that in future all Ministers should travel economy.

Neither Quett nor Tsheko Tsheko touched alcohol so the reception was short lived. We were then each assigned a bodyguard, put in our own black Mercedes limousines and whisked off to Kampala at a breakneck speed in the pitch darkness. When I asked my bodyguard whether we shouldn't slow down a bit he said they were acting under orders because someone had taken a pot shot at their President the previous evening. The next day we were taken to the conference some hundred miles or so west of Kampala. I was booked into a hotel known locally as 'The Dysentery Arms' but the Ministers were more comfortably accommodated. A Tsetse Fly Officer had been instructed to vacate his bungalow for a week and Quett and Tsheko Tsheko were installed in it. The Ugandans attempted to entertain them I believe but one of the Ugandan officials expressed his amazement to me that my Ministers neither drank alcohol nor engaged in casual fornication.

Another election

I was much enjoying my duties in the Ministry of Agriculture but in June 1969 these were severely interrupted. One morning I was told that the President wanted to see me and I was to report to State House immediately. Much puzzled I presented myself and was received in private and most courteously by the President, Sir Seretse Khama. After the usual preliminary courtesies he told me that the second general election would be held on 18 October. This was a closely guarded secret and I wondered why I was being let in on it. The President then went on to tell me what had **not** been done to prepare for the election and my flabbergasted comment was "Bloody hell." He replied "Quite. That is why I want you to take over the arrangements."

It was a tall order. I reported to Tsheko Tsheko who of course was in the know, got a senior administrative officer in the ministry (Ian Gass) to act in my place and set up the elections office the next day and with the help of one of my assistant secretaries (Alan Seager) set about making up for lost time. It was tough going because the general election was to be held on the same day as local government elections and this added to the equipment and staffing requirements. However, both Andrew and I burnt a lot of midnight and weekend oil and the election was held on time and passed off without incident. The ruling party's majority was decreased but it still won 24 out of the 31 seats. The Botswana People's Party retained its three seats. A new party headed by ex Chief Bathoen – the Botswana National Front – captured three seats and the Botswana Independence party that failed in the 1965 election, secured one seat.

Sadly Quett Masire lost to Bathoen largely because although Quett had bravely taken him on in his own stronghold, and even though he was no longer officially chief, he still appealed to the traditionalists in the tribal capital that formed the constituency. The other sad blow was that Tsheko Tsheko lost to Motsamai Mpho of the Botswana Independence Party in the Okavango constituency in the north west because Mpho appealed to his fellow Bayei tribesmen who were in the majority in that area of Ngamiland. Fortunately both of these men were appointed to be members under a constitutional procedure which gave the President discretion to appoint four specially elected members.

To my relief Tsheko Tsheko was re-appointed Minister of Agriculture. Shortly after the elections we went to Rome together for the annual conference of the Food and Agricultural Organisation and I noticed that the Minister was not his old self. He seemed to tire easily and had to miss one or two sessions of the conference. I thought he had perhaps overdone things in his election campaign. Towards the end of the two-week conference he seemed to perk up a bit.

Some time after we returned to Gaborone we decided to tour the Kgalagadi districts and I again noticed that the Minister was not well. He seemed to tire easily but as it was a rather strenuous tour bumping along very rough roads over large distances I thought he would soon recover when we returned to base.

Soon after our return I took a short break with my family up in the far north west in the Okavango. When I returned I was unpacking my car when Richard Mannathoko one of my fellow Permanent Secretaries drew up and told me that Tsheko Tsheko had died earlier that morning. This was a great shock and I wondered whether I should have acted more firmly over what I had thought to be temporary tiredness. He was apparently suffering from very high blood pressure and although he had sought medical advice there was not much that could be done for him. I lost a very good friend and the country a dedicated and able servant. His wife lost a devoted husband. She was devastated and left to care for the seven children.

A new Minister

Amos Dambe was appointed Minister in Tseko Tsheko's place and we got on famously. Amos was an ex teacher. He had been one of the organising brains behind his party's 1965 election campaign and I had got to know him very well then. When Quett moved out of the Prime Minister's office in 1965 to take over the Ministry of Finance there was a slight reshuffle of the ministerial portfolios. Amos who was Minister of Home Affairs moved into Quett's old office which was next to mine and I worked to him.

One morning the Private Secretary to the Queen's Commissioner rang me and said His Excellency was minded to invite the Minister to a dinner part for a visiting French ambassador and wanted to know whether he – the Minister – had a dinner jacket. I replied that I had no idea but I would ask him. The PS was horrified at such indelicacy and told me to hold fire. A short while later the Deputy Queen's Commissioner, Arthur Douglas, telephoned and asked me the same question and I gave the same reply. Arthur said he wasn't sure about my method of finding out about the contents of the Minister's wardrobe and he would ring back. Then it was the turn of the Queen's Commissioner himself to ask whether Amos had a dinner jacket. I was politely exasperated and said the only way I could find out was to ask. Norman Walker asked whether I was sure the Minister would not be offended and I told him to leave it to me. I went in to Amos and in reply to my question he said he was intending to buy one but at present he was without a dinner jacket. I happened to be wearing a jacket so I took it off and asked the Minister to try it for size. It was a good fit and I told him about the dinner party and that he could borrow my evening suit for it. He was delighted and I returned to the telephone and told the Private Secretary to let his master know that the Minister had a dinner jacket.

When the invitation arrived it specified the dress as Black Tie. Amos didn't consult me further but fortunately there was some ceremony or other just before the dinner party which required the attendance of Amos and Seretse. Amos arrived and when I went to receive him I noticed that he looked splendid in my dinner suit but he was wearing a long black tie. Hard on his heels was Seretse with Ruth and I managed a whispered few words with him. He grinned and nodded. After the ceremony I grabbed hold of Amos and we rushed off to my house and we swapped the tie for a tie-on bow tie. We both thought it was a huge joke. One of my friends remarked later that it was my efficiency in dealing with this matter that earned me the MBE.

So Amos and I were old friends. I was amused how he would refer to me in public as "My George". We made many trips together. He was a stickler for standards. I remember him ticking off an expatriate volunteer teacher for appearing before class clad in Bermuda shorts and a brightly coloured shirt. He told him that the children came to school properly dressed and expected their teachers to do the same. He was also very severe to a young veterinary officer who failed to stand when we came into his office. However, our time together was all too short because he was whisked off to the USA to become Botswana's ambassador there.

His place was taken by Edwin Masisi. I had not worked with him before but he was my neighbour and his four year old son and mine used to get up to much mischief together. His boy had an amazing ability to walk on his hands – an athletic feat much admired by my son who was the same age.

I remember going on tour once with the new Minister shortly after his appointment. We went up to Ngamiland in the north west and after our business there decided to cut across the Mababe flats to the Chobe. We stopped for lunch somewhere on the Mababe. After lunch we had been driving for about 20 minutes when the Minister asked from the back seat of the Landrover whether we were going in the right direction. One of our agricultural officers was driving and I made some testy reply. About 10 minutes later the Minister asked us to stop and pointing out a tree to me about a hundred yards off the track said that was where we had taken lunch and he was right. We set off again and kept to the right track this time – our respect for the Minister much increased.

Moving on

In 1972, much as I enjoyed being a Permanent Secretary in Seretse Khama's government I realised that I would have to move on. Although there was absolutely no pressure for me to go, I knew that sooner or later I would have to be replaced by a local officer. I suppose I could have applied for Botswana citizenship and I have every reason to believe that had I done so I would have been granted citizen status. But I did not do so because I am proud of my nationality and could not easily change it much as I loved Botswana. Further to this I had received compensation from the UK for loss of security of office when Bechuanaland became Botswana and it did not seem fair to have one's cake and then expect to be served with more.

So I decided to move on. My staff gave me a farewell present consisting of *The Times World Atlas* and the *Oxford Shorter English Dictionary*. The Government Printer skilfully inserted a page in the latter on which he had printed a quotation from Henry Thoreau chosen by young Andrew Seager which read:

"I left the woods for as good a reason as I went there. Perhaps it seemed to me that I had several more lives to live and could not spare any more time for that one."

I left Botswana with many regrets but I had a young family to support and had to think of its future security. But I had seen the country move from poverty and dependence to relative prosperity and the dignity of independence. It made me proud and still does to think that in some small way I had contributed to building the wonderful Botswana nation.

GLOSSARY

Afrikander	A breed of hump-backed cattle originally bred in South Africa.
Afrikaner	A white native of southern Africa whose mother tongue is Afrikaans.
Biltong	Dried salted meat.
Bushmen	Hunter-gatherers who live in the Kalahari desert and its surrounds.
Cattle kraal	An enclosure for livestock.
Cattle post	An area where cattle are kept around a well or borehole.
Coloured	A person of mixed racial parentage.
Dop	Cape brandy.
Knobkerrie	A stick with a round knob at the end sometimes used as a club or missile.
Kopje	A prominent isolated hill.
Kraal	Sometimes used to describe an African homestead.
Mgakgalagadi	Early inhabitants of Botswana who now survive mainly in the desert areas.
Mokoro	A traditional canoe made from a hollowed out log.
Mophane	A small to medium sized (occasionally large) deciduous shrubby tree.
Pan	A shallow water-filled depression resembling a lake in areas with regular rainfall but usually dry in the desert areas except after heavy rains.
Rhodesia	The former name of Zimbabwe.
Rondavel	A South African word describing a circular, usually thatched, building.
Setswana	The language spoken by the Batswana. It is a Bantu language and uses prefixes and suffixes to modify the meaning of root words. Thus the root word Kgatla becomes Mokgatla when referring to a member of the tribe and Bakgatla in the plural.
South West Africa	Now Namibia.
Stoep	A South African word for a verandah.
Veldt	Elevated open grassland in southern Africa.